TRAUMA REVERSED

PATRICIA I. TILLEY, LMHC

TRILOGY
A WHOLLY OWNED SUBSIDIARY OF TBN
PROFESSIONAL PUBLISHING MEETS POWERFUL PROMOTION

Trilogy Christian Publishers

A Wholly Owned Subsidiary of Trinity Broadcasting Network

2442 Michelle Drive

Tustin, CA 92780

For information, address Trilogy Christian Publishing

Rights Department, 2442 Michelle Drive, Tustin, Ca 92780.

Trilogy Christian Publishing/ TBN and colophon are trademarks of Trinity Broadcasting Network.

For information about special discounts for bulk purchases, please contact Trilogy Christian Publishing.

10 9 8 7 6 5 4 3 2 1

Library of Congress Cataloging-in-Publication Data is available.

ISBN 979-8-89041-503-5

ISBN 979-8-89041-504-2 (ebook)

DEDICATION

This book is dedicated in memory of my beloved mother, Madeline, who was the best mother I could have ever asked for. I am a daughter who is eternally grateful that God gave you to me to be my mother. You will forever be missed. You have imprinted on my heart a legacy of love and faith.

"I remember my mother's prayers, and they have always followed me. They have clung to me all my life."

Abraham Lincoln

ACKNOWLEDGMENTS

I will always remain thankful that my Lord and Savior, Jesus Christ, believed in me. It is an amazing concept that God, Who runs the universe and keeps it all in place, loves me, has had His eye on me my whole life, and has a purpose for me to accomplish. It is the same for you.

I would not have been able to execute His plans without the wonderful family and friends who helped, encouraged, and prayed for me all along. My three terrific sons, David, Steven, and Michael, were very benevolent in making some financial arrangements for me so I could write books. I will forever be full of gratitude and love for them. Thank you, sons! My husband, Jim, saw to it that the errands got run and the yard, house, and dog were taken care of so I could spend a lot of time praying about what the Lord would have me write, do a significant amount of research, and type for many, many hours which turned into months. Family members and friends believed in me and that this book would help many people. On the days I feel computer inept, my son Michael comes to my aid to make the computer "cooperate."

My publisher, Trilogy, and the talented team there made my work look so grand. I appreciate that others who did not know me believed this book of help and my previous book, *Stuff Your Fanny Pack with Coping Skills*, would benefit the multitude.

"The Sovereign Lord has given me an instructed tongue, to know the word that sustains the weary" (Isaiah 50:4, NIV). So, weary or not-so-weary readers, be inspired and receive wisdom. To those who are drained, discontented, taxed, done in, perhaps in several areas of life, take in the words in this book to bring life to every area you need. To God be the glory.

TABLE OF CONTENTS

PREFACE

The statistics for people who have experienced trauma are staggering. That means you are not alone and won't be because I will help you. Hence, this book is written to assist you in healing and move forward. You might feel alone and that nobody understands your pain. But it might not be people who get the hurts you have been through, but certainly the Lord does. He is acutely aware of all your life events, and with that, He has answers. Even if you feel devastated and don't feel like He does understand, go with it, and it will become clearer. Hope is offered. It's a wonderful gift, and we all need it.

What I went through was lengthy, about twelve years of trauma. I went to counseling. Then, I got my degree as a licensed mental health counselor so I could pass on the big nuggets of help. Interestingly enough, I got hired to work for the county's sheriff's department, where I was exposed to some secondary trauma. It became hugely important that I develop even more coping skills for myself, my family, and my clients. My first book, called *Stuff Your Fanny Pack with Coping Skills*, is a result of that, with over five hundred coping skills that work! Now, you can benefit from *Trauma Reversed*. Another collection of coping skills, but this time on overcoming trauma and moving into being a happier, healthier person in spite of what the ugly side of life dished out.

Take a chance on this journey and believe that the God of the universe, Who is able to hold the stars and planets in place, can keep and hold you in place when you feel like you are falling apart. He is that big and certainly that capable. It takes you being willing to let Him. It starts with telling God you will allow His help and will let His love in. Whether beat up emotionally or physically in history, it is still beat up; there is no sugar coating. The pain and sorrow are great. Things didn't go well, so you had to protect yourself. The Lord Jesus is not the One you need to protect yourself from. He is what you need to heal you. I implore you to start with inviting Him in to start your journey to wholeness.

If you are ready, try this prayer:

Dear God,

As I begin this journey to wholeness, I choose to give You every place I have been wounded, including the deepest wounds. I am making the decision not to carry it around with me any longer. It has been like carrying a stinky trash can of hurt. I am letting go of the part of my past that has altered my life dramatically, and I give myself to You, the One Who can re-alter my negative life into something beautiful and positive.

Amen.

By the way, I needed a new clean slate. Start with a new one for yourself as well. The apostle Paul seemed to have weathered it with this scripture:

I know what it is to be in need, and I know what it is to have plenty. I have learned the secret of being content in any and every situation, whether well fed or hungry, whether living in plenty or in want. I can do everything through Him who gives me strength.

Philippians 4:12–13 (NIV)

It's a new day. I am with you to help you in this book, and the Lord brings His presence to all your days and circumstances. His presence is sufficient to meet your challenges. Let's go. Together is better.

Patricia I. Tilley, LMHC

INTRODUCTION

God sees you healed and restored. It is easy to feel like nobody understands what you have been through, and that could be true, but God understands. He offers hope and a way to go forward. Hope has always been there; you just didn't know it or didn't grab onto it. I offer you a truckload of coping skills that work! *Trauma Reversed* is about real help. Even if you think you have tried everything and nothing has caused you to move forward and experience joy again, then rest assured this book is hugely enlightening.

Trauma Reversed works because it came straight from the throne room from the heart of God with you in mind. I listened intently and put creativity to work, adding from my over twenty years of experience skills that have been vital and doable. Scripture is used because it brings life, which is desperately needed, and nature to make it interesting and relatable. My coping skills have helped many people in recovery: those who feel like they are down for the count, those who have suffered so unfairly for years, those who had no idea where to begin to get help, and those who just need some tune-up somewhere as life hit hard and it came so unexpectantly and out of nowhere. It's real self-help, and it's right now in these pages.

Visualize yourself with your very own dump truck. Load it with all the debris/troubles you have. Pretend to get in and drive to your dump site, where you will unload it all. Your truck has a hydraulic cylinder that lifts the bed of the truck to allow the material (your problems) to be dumped. I don't know if the capacity of what is needed for the bed of your truck is for light duty, medium duty, or heavy duty. It doesn't matter. Take as many loads of your problems as needed to that dumpsite. It can take the heaviness of it all. When dumping, say, "I am letting go of my worry, fear, stress, anger, sadness, anxiety, relationship concerns, or history of abuse." You fill in the blank and unload that trauma. Then, breathe in a fresh breath of air. But don't stop there. Where there has been great hurt and angst, skills are needed to keep momentum and learn what it takes to enter into a healthier and happier aspect of life. Trauma took from you, strategies give back.

For those who want to follow after the spiritual dimension, unload your trauma/troubles at the feet of Jesus. First Peter 5:7 (NIV) puts it well: "Cast all your anxiety on Him because He cares for you." This requires action on your part. Just picture the cross with the Lord on it, taking it all for you. Visualize He has answers and a large dose of mercy and grace to replace that heavy burden of life with. He is saying, "I got this daughter or son; receive my peace." The Lord would be okay with the dump truck analogy as well. And again, don't stop there. Trauma stole from you, but the Lord is a giver and a generous one, and He will restore what was stolen. He will because He loves you and wants what is best for you. Read these pages to be part of the solutions in conjunction with allowing God's intervention. It is a win-win as you give it effort and allow the Lord to work what He does best: heal, deliver, revive, and bring His special kind of peace to your heart and mind.

Trauma Reversed has thirty chapters to be your helping hand through the healing process. There are over 400 coping skills, which is a whopping amount of help. You will read about characters such as Annie, the rescue dog; Ellie, the orphaned elephant; a trojan horse, a leech, a creepy angler fish; the monster and the maker; Carl and Camille Camel; and Cindy Cynical Commenter. There is also Sunny Samuel Supporter. You will love reading about how to be a warrior. They are there to remind you what to watch out for and how to be an overcomer.

So, dear readers, delve into these self-help pages and start feeling healthier and on your journey to wholeness and happiness.

Don't forget to get my other book, *Stuff Your Fanny Pack with Coping Skills*. It is also a self-help resource for many of life's challenges. I wish you much growth after your trauma.

"Finally, be strong in the Lord and in His mighty power" (Ephesians 6:10, NIV).

TRAUMA 901

So, you may be wondering what Trauma 901 is. You already know what a Class 101 is. Nine hundred level classes are ones that are independent graduate study, research, thesis, or dissertation. If you have a history of trauma, then you likely have been through Hardship Life Class 101, Misfortune 201, Calamity 301, Misery 401, etc..... You know you could teach about the very tough side of life. I wish it were not so for you. This book comes with help for life on the kinder side, life that has hope, and life lessons to help you heal.

Trauma has no boundaries with age, gender, race, ethnicity, socioeconomic status, or sexual orientation. It is important to talk about and get help to those who are struggling with moving past unhealed trauma. Those who were exposed to trauma have the probability of doubling their risk of having major depressive disorder. That statistic on major depressive disorder is said to affect 11.7 percent of adolescents and 16.6 percent of adults. Trauma exposure is also a requirement to meet the diagnostic statistic manual (DSM-1V) of post-traumatic stress disorder (PTSD). That statistic is 4.7 percent among adolescents and 7.8 percent among adults. Six out of every ten children and one out of two adults in the United States have reported a lifetime trauma experience.[1] So, you are

---

1 National Library of Medicine, *Is developmental timing of trauma exposure associated with depressive and post-traumatic stress symptoms in adulthood?* (January, 2017)

not alone, and you are not going to be alone on your journey to heal. The Lord promises His presence. Know this: His presence is more than enough to meet every challenge.

So, what does a person do when they are at the School of Trauma 901? You have been through some sorrow and suffering with a bumper crop of heartache. Or, at the very least, maybe you were a witness to it. Let me ask you some questions first. Do you want to let go and find freedom from the pain of the past? Have you been stuck with limiting yourself because you thought that was all you deserved? Have you put some heavy judgment on yourself? Are you ready to give up the fear of failing? Would you like to put shame and guilt in its place? I hope that was a yes to all five questions. Good. Let's go! The pages ahead await you.

Pretend that Mr. or Mrs. Trauma is your teacher and you are Stuart Student or Stephanie Student. Your class is "It Is Okay 501." You do need this class to graduate and move on to higher learning. I can call it post-traumatic growth. Trauma taught you that it is okay not to be okay. It's okay to be angry, confused, and disorientated about what happened to you, but make your way to letting things go. It's okay to have some dysfunctional thinking now, as the brain has changed. It's okay that you have been through something and others haven't, and they can't relate but want to be there and want to understand. Let the positive ones in.

It's okay to have scars, but believe they do not define you. It's okay not to feel like you want to take care of yourself, but there will be a test, and to pass it, you have to prioritize yourself. It's okay to feel like quitting, but press through; don't ever give up on yourself. It's okay to have trust issues for now, but you will keep the healing journey going and be wiser. It's okay to feel hopeless for now, but know there are better days coming. Yes, there are. It's a process. When you feel a bit happy one day, embrace it like a ray of sunshine after a severe winter. Look for more. It's okay to feel totally derailed, but be reassured the horror does not define you. It's okay to question God's whereabouts when you had trauma and to ask Him why, but get back to allowing the One who holds the ability to heal you emotionally and physically to have a place in your process. He also loves you fully and will not allow the challenges, difficulties, or even horror to be wasted.

First, make sure you are in a safe place now. If you made it to Class 200–900, then you likely have issues of trust, and it is understandable. Trust was taken away from you, and that is not fair. Trauma is a terrible bully. There is likely betrayal and now shattered beliefs about yourself, others, and the world around you. I am recommending a therapist who specializes in trauma.

To feel safe, a person needs to feel like they will be respected and treated right. Isn't that the opposite of hurting you? You will need to feel like betrayal is the furthest thing from the other person's mind. In order to feel safe again, that person will not want someone to try and control her or him. That means don't allow someone to intimidate you, isolate you, humiliate you, manipulate you, threaten to hurt you, or actually hurt you.

You know your situation and will know when it is safe to leave or if you should stay. Don't put yourself, your children, or your pets at risk. The internet is full of safety planning. Just check into it in case it is needed.

> *"Trauma creates change you do not choose. Healing is about change you do choose."*
>
> **Michelle Rosenthal**

Let's start with ways to feel safe.

SKILLS TO TRY:

1. Grieve your losses. Grieve the way you thought life was going but didn't. Grieve so you can make adjustments to your life that is now altered. There is a mishmash of emotions when life has gone through major changes. You may feel anger and bitterness and have regrets, but to get over it—feel it and accept it. My compassion for you is it is very difficult, but with patience and working on your skills, it is doable.

2. Picture a safe place. That is whatever you deem safe and calming. Maybe it is a room where you had a good memory or a place like a beach. Perhaps it is a thing like a music box that holds a special memory. Picture something comforting with you, such as your pet, stuffed animal, or grandma with you.

3. Surround yourself with people who are safe. These are people that make you feel seen and heard. They would be people with pure intentions.

4. Make your "no" really mean "no." It does not mean maybe. Your body is yours, and nobody gets to touch it without your consent.

5. Set boundaries. It lets others know what you are comfortable with and not comfortable with. Read the section on boundaries.

6. Practice grounding techniques. That means you practice a skill to help you manage anxiety, panic, flashbacks, unwanted memories, or trauma. It will help you to separate from the stress of those things. You are

training the body to get calm. One such skill is to count five things you can see, four things you can hear, three things you can touch, two things you can smell, and one thing you can taste. It keeps you in the moment and may prevent a panic attack.

7. When you feel safe, whether it is feeling safe emotionally or physically, you take back your power from the people who stole it from you. Get a picture of something or someone you consider powerful, and can you depict that as you in some way having a portion of power or strength? Maybe it is a rocket blasting off, a dam holding back millions of gallons of water, the Hulk, or Luisa, the strong woman from the Disney movie *Encanto*. Picturing yourself as being strong will help you build self-esteem and resilience and that "I can do this" attitude.

8. Answer the five questions in paragraph three.

9. How are you doing in class "It Is Okay 501" (paragraph 4)? Check in with yourself. Do you see progress, or are there adjustments to make? Make a plan to adjust.

"May the Lord answer you when you are in distress; may the name of the God of Jacob protect you" (Psalm 20:1, NIV).

The church in Israel was praying this for David as he was preparing for battle. King David was not exempt from distress. We often need the prayers of others, but we shouldn't forget we need to be praying ourselves. Possibly, Jacob was mentioned as God kept him safe in his days of trouble. After all, Jacob's God made him a promise in Genesis 28:15 (NIV), "I am with you and will watch over you wherever you go, and I will bring you back to this land. I will not leave you until I have done what I promised you."

RESPONSE:

_____

_____

_____

_____

_____

_____

_____

_____

_____

_____

_____

_____

_____

_____

_____

_____

_____

_____

_____

_____

_____

ABOUT THOSE THREE FRIENDS

There is nobody, other than the Lord Jesus, who has gone through more trauma than a man in the Old Testament called Job (pronounced "Jobe"). His life was annihilated piece by piece. He had ten children, a wife, eleven thousand animals, many servants, and land/crops. He ended up with one disaster after another as he lost his crops, livestock, and his children. He was also afflicted with painful sores from head to toe. It was noted he was scraping them with a piece of broken pottery. It records in Job 2:13 that his suffering was great. That we can all agree on: it was an over-the-top amount of suffering that would take even the best man or woman down. Job himself states in Job 3:26 (NIV), "I have no peace, no quietness; I have no rest, but only turmoil." That means a state of extreme confusion, agitation, or commotion. That emotional disturbance has anxiety and depression/despair all over it and dosed out to the ultimate degree.

Then you add to that three friends named Eliphaz, Bildad, and Zophar who did some things right and some things wrong. You are looking at this example to learn about what to do right to help someone who has gone through a trauma and things not to do. Let's look at the good things first.

The three friends heard about Job's catastrophes, and they

made a decision to come to him. It is recorded in Job 2:11 that they came to sympathize with him and comfort him. They also saw him and wept loudly (Job 2:12). The friends sat on the ground with him for seven days and nights and did not say a word. I have to give them kudos for sitting on the hard ground for seven days and showing support. All good so far, but there is a but—the negative part. These friends went on and on, as recorded in many chapters, giving so-called advice, adding some berating and speaking erroneously about God, which mounted to what not to say to a traumatized person. They made things worse.

Here are the things to do to help someone who has been through suffering and trauma.

SKILLS TO TRY:

1. Show up. At least the three men came and showed solidarity. Just the showing up part is reassuring that you are there for the friend. They let Job mourn. They were very solid with their presence until they started speaking.

2. Offer appropriate sympathy and compassion. They wept with their friend. I recall a time when a very dear friend of mine lost her son. When I saw her, I cried as I was so full of sorrow for her loss.

3. The three friends had to be uncomfortable as they sat on the ground for what I would consider a significant amount of time. Tragedy does not come when it is convenient, and it may be physically and emotionally challenging for helpers. How could it not? If it is not a good time or easy to accomplish to get to the person who needs consoling, then try your best to show your support. Even if you can't be there in person, offering

support via the computer, texts, or calls is still support.

4. A friend or family member will have bad days. Just allow for them. It's part of the process.

5. Try getting your person moving and doing activities they enjoy. This will stimulate the feel-good hormones. But no pushing.

6. Help them look at who are the positive/stable people in their life. Encourage them to connect with them.

7. Educate yourself and your person with ways to ease the stress and trauma. Educate yourself with what to expect and inform your person that their journey to healing is a process. Your attempts to try to understand will come across that you care.

8. Validate their feelings. Accept them. They feel what they feel. It is an individual journey, and everyone processes the trauma differently.

9. Be patient. You may think you know what they need, but they might not know what they need and most likely will need time to come to that conclusion. Their reactions are normal for what they have been through. Don't take things personally.

10. Practice self-care for yourself, as helping others can be draining. This will include you acknowledging your own feelings about what happened to your person. This may be your anger and sadness over their event.

11. Help your person learn to relax. Suggest ways to practice self-care. Read the sections in this book on self-care.

12. Help them resolve day-to-day issues so things don't pile up and cause additional stress and worry.

13. Listen and listen some more. Talking can be very hard for the trauma survivor.

14. Giving advice may need to be as asked for.

15. Help them increase any safety concerns.

16. Encourage them to keep a routine and participate in habits that are healthy and enjoyable.

17. See if there are tangible things you can do to be helpful, such as bring a dinner in, do chores, pick up the kids from school, or get them to their ballgames or music practice.

18. Take the situation seriously. If the person who experienced the trauma wants to talk, then follow their lead and make sure they are comfortable.

19. Respect their need for space and privacy. Actually, that can be healthy as people need to collect their thoughts.

20. Let the afflicted person make the decisions according to what they think is best. They will know if they can go out, drive, go to certain places, etc.. It is their life, so give them control over it. The exception is if they feel like they would hurt themselves or someone else. Step in if you see they are deteriorating. If they say they are not ready for something, then respect that.

21. Ask if you can pray for the hurting person. Pray with love and hope behind the words.

22. As time passes, don't forget to keep following up with the traumatized person. Time does not heal all wounds.

23. Don't try to fix your loved one. They will do the work little by little, step by step. Just love them. There is a lot of pain, and they need time.

24. Trust issues may appear now when it was not a concern before. Remember, it's not about you. You may be totally trustworthy, but it will not be easy for your loved one. Something happened, and the brain has been rewired.

25. Make sure your loved one knows The National Suicide Prevention Lifeline 1-800-273-8255 or text HOME to 741741. Since July 2022, all calls and text messages to 988 are routed to a suicide and crisis lifeline. 988 is an easier number to remember.

So, there are the "dos," and of course, there are the "don'ts." Job told the friends in Job 16:2–3 (NIV), "I have heard many things like these; miserable comforters are you all! Will your long-winded speeches never end? What ails you that you keep on arguing?" Oh my, being called "miserable comforters." It is true, but it stings.

The friends did come with a good intention to comfort, but they missed the mark. Having friends like that is like living with a snake. You can live with a snake, but you never know when it will bite you. Long "take to task" speeches when you are hurt emotionally and physically are the last on my list of helpfulness. The speeches were needless and useless. They would be like rubbing salt in a hurting person's wounds.

For Job, the miserable comforters were people. Consider if it is not actual people who are "miserable comforters" but just the wrong kind of comforters. An example would be having Donald Downhearted as a comforter who is busy drowning himself in something addictive, or Pamela Promiscuous engaging with many partners to numb the pain. Don't let Cora Complainer get near you, as she will shred any little bit of good vibes you are trying to hang on to. I would not enjoy Porter Poorthing coming around and making me the object of pity. Consider if you are comforted by social media in excess. These situations are ways that you decide to manage trauma, such as escaping, feeling like you want wanton risky relationships, or zoning out and causing brain fog and detachment.

> *"I am not what happened to me. I am what I chose to become."*

Carl Jung, founder of analytical psychology

SKILLS TO AVOID AND THINGS TO NOT SAY TO THE TRAUMATIZED PERSON:

1. Don't judge. People usually do not have all the facts. Making a bad judgment is like putting others down. It boils down to self-exultation when you do that. We never know what a person has been through, what they are going through currently, and how experiences, in this case severe trauma, have affected their life. Support is merciful; judging is negative. The person you are judging will likely feel like that is what you are doing—judging and making them feel blamed, demoralized, and victimized. Acceptance is of huge importance.

2. Don't pity the person. Compassion would be the opposite. Offering compassion means to "suffer together." It makes you want to do something to relieve their suffering. Be kind, empathetic, and understanding. After all, something has devastated your loved one.

3. In your curiosity, be careful with the questions you ask. If you ask, "Why didn't you call?" or "Why did you go

there?" it just causes a person to be on the defensive, and they will feel like you are discrediting their intelligence and decision-making. You will sound like you are blaming them for what happened.

4. Try not to take control. They may already feel like power or control was exercised over them.

5. Be very careful with saying, "You know how it feels." You may have had a similar event happen to you, but people are in different places emotionally and physically, and one can't fully know how a person feels. It usually comes across as shame or blame to them.

6. There is a fine line between allowing the person to talk about the event and being able to handle what is said and their reaction and not insisting that they talk. Ask if they want to talk. If they don't want to talk to you, then see if they prefer a different person. Don't be dismissive. They may also wonder if anyone will believe them.

7. Don't ever say, "You're lucky that such and such didn't happen," or "You need to move on." Don't tell the survivor to try and be strong or that it's time to get over it. Don't tell them to look on the bright side. Do not ever say, "It could not have been that bad." Never tell them to "let it go." All of that is very insensitive and shows a big lack of understanding of suffering.

8. Avoid calling someone a victim. That word denotes something negative for the most part. It makes the person who had a traumatic event feel helpless and weak, and it may cause them to feel guilt and shame. The court system will use the word "victim" as part of the

criminal justice system, but if you are connected with a person who had a trauma, say "survivor." That will help the afflicted individual feel empowered and that they did survive and may be moving into the healing process.

9. Don't assume that everyone who has been through a trauma needs professional help. But, have available resources/numbers if the person decides this for themselves.

"A word aptly spoken is like apples of gold in settings of silver" (Proverbs 25:11, NIV).

Aah, the perfect word spoken to someone who needs comfort after a loss or a personal trauma shows understanding and care. It is really like a comparison that the comforting, well-spoken word is like something of beauty.

RESPONSE:

_____

_____

_____

_____

_____

_____

_____

_____

_____

_____

_____

_____

_____

_____

_____

_____

_____

_____

_____

_____

_____

_____

_____

_____

TRY A LITTLE DETECTIVE WORK

*"A bird sitting on a tree is never afraid of the
branch breaking because her trust is not
on the branch but on her own wings.
Always believe in yourself."*

Charles Wardle

There are many challenges for the person who has been through a traumatic event, but the one that is in particular difficult to get through is to regain trust. That is trust in themselves and trust in others. The statistics for the number of adults in the US who have experienced some type of traumatic event at least once in their lives is 70 percent, or 223.4 million people. That is a huge number of people who will all need to go through the process of regaining trust again.

The traumatic event took from you, for one thing, your feeling of being safe. It left you with pain and heartache, and you may have no idea how to get joy back in your life. Your loss has left you numb. You will get through it; yes, you will. Never, ever think you deserved any of that pain. You have a greater sense of fear now because your brain has been rewired. It is about self-preservation, so you will do your ultimate best to never allow hurt again. It's not a bad thing.

To trust yourself again requires you to give yourself compassion and love. There is to be no beating yourself up. Seriously, forget healing if that's what you are all about. How you talk to yourself matters. If you talk to yourself with empathy, you will get to the place of trusting yourself again. Dismiss your inner critic. Be patient, it just takes time. It is not like the post office, which can do overnight deliveries. So, no rush job. It will be way past overnight. Know what you need and say what you need. That "talking to you" that you want to do to yourself should include phrases of "You are okay, you are human," not put-downs. This period where you are trying to heal will be a time to build resiliency and courage. You are smarter now. Say "no" when you want to say "no." Encourage yourself and say encouraging things to yourself, and you will see your self-esteem improve. You will have to trust yourself that you are worthy and will be okay, then more than okay—happy once again.

> *"Instead of saying, 'I'm damaged, I'm broken, I have trust issues,' I say I'm healing. I'm rediscovering myself. I'm starting over."*

> **Horacio Jones**

Trusting in other people again requires you to be vulnerable, and that's a tough one. It's because you think, "Well, I did that and saw what happened; I won't do that again." You have chosen not to risk it. But you can do this. Be like Sherlock Holmes and look carefully for clues of how people have been with you in the past and how people are now. What have they said and done? Are the facts accurate, or are you just feeling the hurt? Are they being honest, but you didn't like the truth? Are they reliable, responsible, fair, dependable, keep your confidence, and keep their promises as best as possible? Sherlock Holmes, a very famous fictional detective, was very observant and asked a lot of "whys." People who are

34

hurting seem to jump to the wrong conclusion and miss that there are people in their past and present who are worthy to be trusted.

So, when attempting to trust again, take your time about it; have some skills to assist you. Be a sleuth, not oblivious; be cautious, not reckless; be shrewd, not naïve; be vigilant, not inattentive; be careful, not careless; be meticulous, not negligent; be of sound mind, not paranoid, and be courageous, not fearful.

Your intuition is a very good guide and a gift from God. Oxford Dictionary reports that intuition is the ability to understand something immediately, without the need for conscious reasoning.[2] It seems to help us know things, and it will help a person move towards or away from people. For those who make choices to listen to the Holy Spirit, go with it definitely. God is guiding you. Holy Spirit is causing your intuition to become acute. For example, you meet somebody you are beginning to like, and your intuition is sending up red flags, and you find out later that intuition was right as they are a womanizer or femme fatale. You are desperate for a ride home as your car is in the shop, and your co-worker offers. That person is nice enough to work with, but your intuition smells a rat. They had an ulterior motive. That uneasy feeling is a warning. Listen to it! Pay attention, especially when you feel troubled. Don't ignore God's voice, as He has your safety in mind always. As you are relearning to trust people again, listen to intuition and to God's still, small voice. I cannot count how many times I have been protected by listening to the wisdom of God and my intuition. My mother raised me with "If in doubt, don't." Over the many years, I have learned to listen to the Holy Spirit. I quite accurately hear that still, small voice saying, "Don't go today, go tomorrow," or to call a certain person, or "Don't say anything about such and such." I love it when I hear very clearly to pray for someone and

---

2 "Intuition." Intuition, noun—Definition, pictures, pronunciation and usage notes | Oxford Advanced Learner's Dictionary at OxfordLearnersDictionaries.com. Accessed September 3, 2023. https://www.oxfordlearnersdictionaries.com/definition/english/intuition.

later learn they were in a crisis at that time.

SKILLS TO TRY:

1. Stop for a moment and listen to your inner voice. Is it judging, name-calling, expressing disapproval, or is it unfairly negative? It seems to dog you with "Why didn't you?" or "That was messed up," or "You're messed up." Does it make you feel worthless? First of all, be aware of that inner critic, as in what it is saying and what the scenario is. Then get yourself calm, as your nervous system will appreciate you doing this. That negative barrage is not your intuition or the Lord. Now, replace that with something kind you would say to yourself. That inner critic will hurt your ability to get motivated to do anything, let alone trust again. It is too busy pointing out your weakness. Kick Cynthia Cynical Commenter to the curb. Invite Sunny Sammy Supporter to go hand in hand with you.

2. Develop your intuition. That's your gut, really. When listening to the still, small voice of the Lord, you should get peace. That's your barometer. He will give you promptings, impressions, and reminders. He has your best interest at heart. Get your emotions to quiet down so you can hear that voice. Be desirous of hearing God. God's voice will go higher and deeper than intuition.

3. Pay attention to red flags. You do have common sense, so listen to it. If those red flags are glaring, move away from what is trying to do wrong to you. The red flags are warnings that something is dangerous, unhealthy, or manipulative. The red flags say "risk," and they say

"pay attention." If a person is ignoring the red flags, there is likely insecurity, and they may have a fear of abandonment.

4. Jesus said in Mark 4:9 (ESV), "He who has ears to hear let him hear." So, in essence, if you are listening, you will gain understanding. It is better to be safe than sorry.

5. Set boundaries. It is a violation of trust if someone does not respect your boundaries. Make sure you state what your boundaries are. Boundaries let others know you have rules that must be followed to show respect for yourself and others. See the chapter on boundaries.

6. Looking for clues like a detective may just be the thing to keep you away from negative and dangerous people, places, and things. Even salt can deceptively look like sugar. That means be cautious as not everything is as it seems. I don't want your sugar bowl to have salt in it. Detectives find clues that others overlooked. You can do this.

"Be very careful, then, how you live—not as unwise but as wise, making the most of every opportunity, because the days are evil. Therefore, do not be foolish, but understand what the Lord's will is" (Ephesians 5:15–17, NIV).

The Apostle Paul says to not just be careful but very careful and to be wise. We all need this reminder, which is essentially saying to not be without reason, as well as to look around before taking a step. Walk out your Christian walk with wisdom. To make the most of every opportunity means to be good stewards of your time and put value on it. Recognize opportunities and seize the moment. Redeem the time and prioritize things that are important.

Paul was saying the days are evil because, at the time, there was a lot of persecution and opposition; there are dark days now as well. For God's will to be understood is to read His word and seek Him. He delights in telling His people direction and His will.

RESPONSE:

_____

_____

_____

_____

_____

_____

_____

_____

_____

_____

_____

_____

_____

_____

_____

_____

_____

_____

_____

_____

HEED THE ROAD SIGNS

Pretend you are in a very nice vehicle and want to drive it, but you can't drive it. It's not that there is a mechanical issue or there is no gas, but something else is driving your vehicle. It's your feelings. Your vehicle is your life, and your feelings have been driving your life all around. They have stopped you all over the place from recovering from trauma.

Let's look at the most common feelings as road signs. There is "the yield" sign, which means to slow down and check traffic in all directions. It should alert you that drivers and pedestrians are out there. Your yield is your caution. Don't repeat the same mistakes. That does not mean that what happened to you was your fault by any means, but be wise and alert and watch for traps and triggering events.

There is the "stop" sign. It should be obvious that it means stop—come to a complete stop. That is not a Hollywood stop, as in rolling through slower, but stop means stop. This analogy means stop with the wrong thinking. Maybe you don't know you are thinking wrong. Perhaps you are so used to listening to your critical voice. You must stop negative self-talk. That inner critic has put you down, judged you unfairly, criticized you mercilessly, and made sure to point out your faults. In actuality, it has taken a toll on your ability to get well. Hence the stop sign, which means to stop doing that!

There could be a "do not enter" sign. It means just that: do not enter. But it also means you went the wrong way. That could mean that opposing traffic could be coming towards you. It is better to heed that as you want to surely stay away from opposing people. Hopefully, you recognize Mary Manipulative, Thaddeus Threatening, Ines Intimidation, Preston Pressuring, Vincent Violent, Abby Abusive, and Colton Coercion. Definitely watch the "do not enter" signs. High-tail it away.

Trauma makes you feel helpless. That means the feeling you can't do anything to help yourself. You may not have the strength or power to do anything for yourself or do anything for anyone else, which could be your children. You feel defeated and that you should just accept this detrimental condition. It could also be that the trauma you experienced has caused you to not even go out of your house. It is like the "dead-end" sign. It lets the driver know that the road they are on ends in a dead end.

Trauma makes you feel like you have lost control. This can be so overwhelming that you can't find your way or who you are anymore. Your self-esteem takes a big hit. I am calling this the "private road, no trespassing" sign. It means someone has remained on your property without permission. Well, maybe you gave permission because you felt like you had no other alternatives. But some manipulator trespassed on you and yours. It is a sign to prevent intruders from being on your property (or on you). There is a caveat that, hopefully, you gave warnings and set boundaries on what was and was not permissible.

If you survived a trauma, you most likely have trust issues. Do not worry; this is a regular feeling. Understandably, how can a person feel safe? It causes feelings of vulnerability. Feeling like you will be betrayed or in harm's way is most common. I am calling this sign "slow, congested area." The reason is it feels crowded, blocked, and confused in one's head. The slow part is just that—it takes time to regain feeling resilient again. It takes time to feel like you will not be in danger with a person. It takes time to believe if other people will have your back or they will bolt for the door when they don't like something about you. Emotionally trusting someone needs to be earned. Time is the gift here.

Feeling hopeless is a tough feeling of a road sign. I will call this road sign "construction ahead." The sign is there to let the driver know that possible dangerous conditions are near. It could be hazardous. It is usually temporary. Well, that part is up to you. Don't ever feel hopeless! There is always hope because the Lord is over the entire universe. He makes a way when it looks like there is no way. He is aware of you. Ask Him for help. As the sign says, it could be hazardous. If you stay in hopelessness, it can lead to despair and suicidal ideation. The literal road sign would be an indicator to be aware of machinery, debris, people working, smoke, uneven roads, etc. So, a detour may be needed. If you feel hopeless, then definitely a detour is needed. My detour recommendation is to a mental health professional if things are not manageable and are overwhelming. You could use some assistance to get to your House of Healing on Recovery Road.

There is one more very important road sign for now, and that is a "flagger ahead" sign. With all due respect and for illustration purposes, I am calling the Lord Jesus our "flagger." A flagger ahead sign is used to warn drivers that a flagger is controlling traffic. The job is to help direct traffic safely through the work zone and thus to stop or slow down. I'm sure you get it that the Lord is present "on the road of life with us," controlling our traffic emotionally, physically, mentally, socially, financially, relationally, and spiritually. In listening to His direction, we must stop or slow down as

He always has our safety and well-being in His heart and is fully aware of what lies ahead.

SKILLS TO TRY:

1. The yield road sign is your warning to be wary of traps and retriggering events. That means something, "a trigger," has caused a painful memory to resurface. It's about your own experience, so it could be about anything. It's about reliving the painful event. Know what your triggers are. The key is to calm your nervous system. Pay attention to what is happening in your body, such as suddenly having anxiety, feeling panic, muscle tension, sweating, or having a faster heart rate. Do you cry and feel overwhelmed? It's about bringing you back to the present so you don't feel overwhelmed. Be sure to soothe yourself.

2. Take a break, slow down, deep breathe and recharge. Have a friend or family member that you can connect with and tell them you are reacting to something intense from your past. If you know of a possible trigger situation coming up, then tell them ahead of time and give them strategies that work when you feel so emotionally uncomfortable.

3. The stop sign is to remind you to stop all the negative self-talk. Gees, how could you possibly feel like you are recovering when you listen to and even agree with the critical voice that berates you at every chance? This really does take practice and time. Bad Buddy Belittling needs to be eliminated. Be aware of that condemning voice and tell yourself they are thoughts, not facts about yourself.

4. Pause and breathe. You need the time to rethink and calm your nervous system so you can realize that Felicity Fault Finding is nit-picking and is not accurate. Counteract the critical voice with something true and positive. For example, there is no evidence to support the critic saying, "You are stupid."

5. Do something physical. Change gears to moving so you concentrate on the physical activity, not on Judith Judging.

6. That "do not enter" sign is a reminder to avoid people who are all wrong for your mental and physical well-being. Who are those people in your life? Some may be recognizable in the above paragraph. How do they make you feel when you are around them? Do you feel like you walk on eggshells or you cannot turn your back? Are you experiencing unwanted touching, pressure, or guilt trips for sexual favors? Are the children being used as pawns? Are you being told you deserve the abuse? Are you forced to be separated from family and friends? Are you scared? Have you had to watch your partner punch things, show weapons, or make faces that are meant to intimidate you? Are you being humiliated, insulted, or embarrassed? I do understand that you may live with someone who is toxic to you. It may be tough to make the decision to leave an unhealthy relationship, especially if you are economically dependent on that person. Make careful and wise decisions. The timing of this is critical.

    If you have been bitten enough in your scummy alligator pond, make realistic plans to get to a healthier pond. You are experiencing more damage or brokenness by staying. Get support to help you move on, and don't try to keep the negative relationship after you have made a break. If you are being abused emotionally, physically, or sexually, remember there are shelters. Check your area. Be careful as loneliness sets in and, at other times, relief sets in. Loneliness needs to be managed as it can cause you to return to what is negative. Get a whole handful of coping skills to not fall prey to its trap. It is better to be a healthy single than the abused one in a duo.

7. The "dead-end" sign is a sign that you are experiencing helplessness. It's a terrible feeling. You are unhappy and down so low you can only see your shoelaces. Identify where this feeling is coming from. What is on your mind? Are you focusing on what is uncontrollable? Look at what is in your power to change. Look at where you are capable and strong. Empower yourself. Depression is most likely part of feeling helpless. Consider seeing a mental health professional. You deserve a break from the tough stuff.

8. The "private road, no trespassing" sign has been ignored. If you set any boundaries, they were not respected. You should be able to tell other people what your needs are. It is okay if you want to say "no." It is okay to set and practice what are your values. If you are having a hard time setting boundaries, then take some time to see if it is because you could be a people pleaser or fear rejection or possible putdowns.

9. The "slow, congested area" sign is just that. Time is needed. Losing trust and being betrayed is like a kick in the gut. The first step to recovery is to stop hanging with the terrible, toxic, harmful, septic system people.

Look at number six above. How about looking around seriously for helpful, kind, and harmless connections? Confusion happens because you don't know what or who can be trusted. You feel stuck and vulnerable. The decision is whether or not you are actually in a decent relationship and understanding and forgiveness are needed, or it's a negative relationship, and you need out. Examine what went wrong. You get to decide if the offender should have a second chance. Listen to each other and what is needed. It is okay to move on. On a personal note, I received someone in my house that stole jewelry from me. It took two years before I felt like I could trust that person in my house again.

10. A construction ahead sign is helpful if heeded. It's a warning, but some are doing their own thing, feel indifferent, or think they can just get by. The sign is there to help maintain safety. How is that working so far in your relationships? Are you happy, fulfilled, emotionally comfortable, and safe? Have doubt, worry, and fear dogged you? Does your soul feel alive? Probably, you do feel some hopelessness, which means you do not believe life can get better. It is imperative that when life has gone all in the opposite direction, you hang onto hope. You must believe that things can get better. You must be careful that your mind has not turned your situation into something worse than it is. Self-care is huge. You cannot believe anything good can happen, but keep hope before you by writing down some possibilities. These might be hope to keep working or get an even better job, have better relationships come into your life, or your children to do well in school, etc....
Is there anything that is making the feeling of hopelessness worse? That could include using drugs or

alcohol, staying in bed all day, not practicing appropriate hygiene, any self-harm behaviors, or hanging with people who abuse you. Change what you are doing that is dragging you down the slippery slope of gloom and doom. Do not accept any resignation of this being all there is. Refute that with all your might! A quality support system should be able to help you if you tell them about your despair. The suicide prevention hotline is 1-800-273-8233 or 988.

11. And, of course, one should never ignore the "flagger" sign. For all intents and purposes, the flagger, in my case, the Lord Jesus, is in charge, giving warnings for what lies ahead. Don't be alone driving all over, crossing the line, going almost in the ditch, and nearly hitting the trees and concrete. The Lord loves you and wants to help you get through life. Because He loves us, He wants what's best for us; because He knows us, He knows what is best for us; and because He is all-powerful, He has the ways and means to bring it all about. If you are trusting Him, continue even more so where there have been struggles, and if you are not trusting that He is benevolent to you in all areas, please consider allowing God to help you. A spiritual advisor would be helpful.

"Then they cried to the Lord in their trouble, and He saved them from their distress. He brought them out of darkness and the deepest gloom and broke away their chains" (Psalm 107:13–14, NIV).

What good news! It is especially good news for anyone who feels like they have chains on. If you notice part A, where it says they cried to the Lord, they came to God, and then in part B, He saved them from their distress, brought them out of darkness and gloom, and broke their chains. Sounds like a very solid plan. If you are not making any progress emotionally with where you want to be in life, feel that nothing works, and your life is a dead end, then try part A.

RESPONSE:

_____

_____

_____

_____

_____

_____

_____

_____

_____

_____

_____

_____

_____

_____

_____

_____

_____

_____

_____

_____

THE MONSTER
AND THE MAKER

This interesting title refers to Frankenstein as the maker and his created monster, who had no official name other than creature, fiend, devil, or ogre. So, are you wondering what this has to do with trauma? People who have gone through traumatic experiences normally have feelings of guilt and shame. Guilt is about something you did but should not have or didn't do but should have, and shame is about who you are. Guilt involves one's negative attitude or behavior. Shame involves one feeling inadequate, flawed, worthless, or a "bad person." The guilt feeling lets you know you need to make the situation right, which ultimately will make you feel better about yourself.

The connection between trauma and guilt is that a person has a very uncomfortable feeling as they feel like they should have done something different at the time of their traumatic experience. An example could be something that happened on the battlefield, a work scenario, leaving the scene of an accident, or not attempting to leave an abusive situation or report it.

If you are experiencing guilt, then examine if you beat yourself up a lot, have a lot of doubts and regrets, can't forgive yourself, feel that you let other people down, or don't live up to your responsibilities. Then there are those things you wish you had not said but don't make amends or apologize if possible.

The connection between trauma and shame is that the person who has gone through a traumatic event often blames themselves. It causes deep, destructive feelings of being flawed, unlovable, unworthy, and purposeless. It is especially difficult for the person who has been sexually assaulted or abused as a child or by an intimate partner. These survivors often want to slip into oblivion. That feeling of powerlessness is intense, and with it comes Ernie Evaluator, the negative cousin whose job is to make you feel like you will never feel better. Ultimately, you end up with depression, anxiety, withdrawal, and pushing people who are trying to help away. A person who is struggling with shame feels like they don't know where to go to feel safe.

Going back to our monster and the maker. Victor Frankenstein, a character from a novel and movie by Mary Shelley, is a scientist obsessed with trying to recreate life. He does create a monster and then feels guilt for creating him as the monster turns destructive and murderous. Guilt makes a person feel troubled with their emotions where they have feelings of conflict. Frankenstein had regret and anguish at what he had created. He was deeply depressed and disgusted as well. He chose to abandon the monster when the monster needed him. He acted selfishly. He broke his promise to the beast as he did not build a mate for him.

The monster felt lonely, and his self-evaluation was that he was malicious, miserable, and shunned. He was constantly rejected and looked upon with disgust. He was also very depressed and felt betrayed because Frankenstein left him. His remorse was palpable. He had been beaten after doing a good thing of saving a girl from drowning. There are many layers to shame, and it is difficult to unravel and heal from. He started out in baby ways, like being loving and kind, but with the way he was treated, he ended up revengeful, bitter, angry, and felt unacceptable and deserving of disdain. It is a very sad tale on both accounts of what guilt and shame can do to a person.

Let's change gears and look at a couple of examples from the Bible that are not fiction, as just described. Back in the Bible times, if you were childless, society made you feel ashamed and disgraced. In Genesis 30, there is an exchange of handmaidens several times in hopes that pregnancies would result. Childlessness caused feelings of hopelessness, worthlessness, and failure. In fact, the more children a woman had, the better her position.

There was another example of shame in 2 Samuel 9. It's the story of King David and Mephibosheth (Muh-fib-uh-sheth). He is the son of King David's best friend, Jonathan, and grandson of King Saul. His father and grandfather died in a battle, and as a result, the child's nurse fled in an attempt to help Mephibosheth escape from who would be the new ruler. The nurse either accidentally dropped him or he fell and, as a result, broke his bones, leaving him crippled in both feet. Mephibosheth had been living as an outcast, and when King David inquired if he could do any acts of kindness for anyone left in the household of Saul, his name was reported. When he was summoned, he responded with fear and asked the king a question: "What is your servant that you should notice a dead dog like me?" This poor crippled boy felt like he was going to die, as it was the norm when a new king took over to eliminate any remaining family of the outgoing king. I can't help but think so highly of King David that he wanted to show kindness to this boy. After all, the child had basically been forgotten and lived in desolation. Kindness is such a wonderful expression of the character of the Lord Jesus. Think about it: we were weak and broken, and yet God drew us to Himself and made a place for us at His table.

How is this a story of shame? In those days, society did not treat crippled people well. It was unfavorably looked at as to have any disability. Sometimes, the indifference even turned to violence. There was no pride in the family unit, and they were excluded from holy places. That is a terrible commentary. It is also a sad commentary for today as many with disabilities live with shame because of misunderstandings, ignorance on others' part, discrimination, and stereotypes (presumptions). May it not be so! Yet, I know it is. When this happens, the disabled person may push people away so they do not feel rejected or humiliated. Since shame makes one feel self-conscious, there is a host of other emotions that go with it, such as self-judgment, pain, trust issues, and powerlessness. With any disability, we would be safe to say there most likely has been trauma. It is different for each one and to different degrees.

SKILLS TO TRY:

1. Stop playing negative events and mistakes over and over in your mind. If you can become aware when the negative thought comes up, then you can challenge it. Tell yourself that does not feel true. An example is if the critical voice tells you that you are a failure, then you counteract it with: "There is no evidence to support that; it's a lie." The truth can be greater than the shame. Ask yourself where that negative voice is coming from. Could it be the devil whispering that you are worthless, or could it be from childhood where a voice has been dogging you with "You will never amount to anything?" In either case, rebuke it or discredit it with the truth.

2. Self-forgiveness is a big deal. The human side of us is about making mistakes and making amends with others

we may have harmed. But it also includes forgiving yourself. Practice self-acceptance.

3.   Change the picture of yourself. Something happened in your history. That's all of us. Some harm may have occurred. What can you do to see yourself in a more positive light now? Tell yourself you are growing, more respectful, more enlightened, more mature now, etc.... Many people have an inaccurate view of themselves. Now focus on today, good plans for tomorrow, and positive things that you have planned for the next week, month, and year. Do not see yourself as Guilty Glenda, but Enrique Enlightened. Change the pic of yourself from Shawn Shame to Robert Respect. Pick your name. For example, I am not Pathetic Pat or Poor Pat but Powerful Pat.

4.   Some people think you should "pay" for what has happened. Do your best to make all needed amends, then avoid the people who want you to stay down the slippery sliding slope called stuck. Drop the people who don't give two hoots about you and prefer to see you fry. Not everyone will care, and that is okay. Find those who do care.

5.   Sometimes, when guilt shows up, it is really a different feeling that you are dealing with. Examine if it is anger, low self-esteem, jealousy, frustration, disappointment, or any number of other feelings. Ask yourself if your guilt is because you don't think you deserve anything good. Change that to you deserving a second or third chance. You are not bad to the bone.

6.   Talk to others who you trust and those who can be honest with you. I would ask, "Do you think I was mean to

so and so?" or "Do you see me as a person who breaks my promises too often?" or "Has my behavior been reckless over the last few weeks?" If it was something that was done to you, then oftentimes, sharing with understanding others will make you feel less hurt. Make the necessary changes.

7.   Grieve your experience. The process of grief helps you accept the loss(es) and move forward with your life. We are human, so we must feel those feelings to move through the trauma. It may be anger, sadness, anxiety, numbness, confusion, or bitterness. You may have the feelings from the aftermath of the trauma for a very long time, but eventually, they will be less intense. Grieving has a purpose, and that is to get you to a place of living healthy and happy again. If that does not happen, then a counselor can help with what could be complicated or traumatic grief.

8.   I keep saying the importance of self-care because it is so true. We must take care of ourselves. Give yourself some compassion. Tell yourself it is okay to feel better.

9.   Do for others. There is something about taking your mind off your own trauma and drama. It feels good to help other people or animals. Maybe it is about volunteering and checking on other people's welfare. You will be making connections and new friends, and quite possibly, someone can relate to you. It certainly will take your mind off your circumstances, your loss, and your pain and add some "zippity doo dah" to your otherwise stress-filled day. The reward center of your brain will be stimulated, and you naturally will begin to feel better. Feelings of benevolence to others will fill you

up instead of having hours of "woe is me."

10. If you have a disability or you are interacting with someone with a disability, please ask before you step in, as they may be able to or just want to do whatever themselves. Never be patronizing or show pity. We are all humans who want to be treated with dignity and respect. Focus on one's abilities, not their disabilities. Be very careful of the language you use. For example: don't say words like "handicapped," say "person with a disability"; don't say "dwarf or midget," say "person who is small in stature"; don't say "retarded," say "person with a cognitive disability"; and don't say "cripple," say "person who needs mobility assistance." If a person dealing with disabilities has any shame or feels stigmatized, then showing respect goes a long way to show the person that they have value. If you have a disability, give yourself the respect you deserve. Love yourself and give honor to yourself. In fact, if you dole out the self-love and respect, I expect you will find the confidence to kick shame to the curb. You can be proud of who you are and still have flaws. We all have flaws. When you respect yourself, you will deal with any misgivings on your part and will not tolerate it in others. Well, at least you can appropriately let someone know what is unacceptable.

11. Attitude is everything. Maybe you have some guilt and shame that attached itself to you like super glue, but with the right attitude and skills you apply, you will see self-growth and can conquer the past and start feeling that you have worth. You are important no matter your history. Be your own inspiration no matter what.

12. Have something healthy that drives you. Develop your skills. Work hard. Exercise to deal with any pent-up negative energy. Improve the parts of your personality that may be challenging. I am not saying to change your identity, but if you have an impatient side or you tend to be hard-nosed or snarky, work on it. People will enjoy the social interactions with you much more, and you will begin to see you are noticed, wanted, and liked/loved.

13. Mephibosheth felt like a dead dog. What does that mean to you? It may mean he felt worthless, disgraced, insignificant, humiliated, helpless, broken and crippled. He lost his father and grandfather when he was very young. With the escape came the unknown and not living with all his needs being met. And suddenly, the healthy child became lame. The future looked bleak. There was fear. By the way, a dog in the Bible was considered an unclean animal and one who was a roaming scavenger. Can you relate to Mephibosheth? His self-esteem was low to the ground. But, being a dog lover, let me interject what a dog displays: strength, courage, tenacity, love, faithfulness, unselfishness, intelligence, patience, and companionship. So, forget about any "dead dog mentality" and develop good qualities that build yourself up.

14. With guilt, change your behavior so as not to repeat what brought on the guilt again. If you see a negative pattern, work on it and learn from it. Admit what you did and examine why you did what you did. Make amends if possible. Do you want to tailor yourself to the person you want to be? If so, make a doable plan and possibly incorporate support for help and accountability.

"As the scripture says, "Anyone who trusts in Him will never be put to shame" (Romans 10:11, NIV).

This is simple yet powerful. Trusting in the One who is trustworthy is the way towards the journey of healing. The Lord even knows how to vindicate your life. That means to clear someone of blame. This trust in the Lord also means to trust Him for salvation; thus, you will not be put to shame. You will not be disgraced. That is an offer that is very hard to turn down.

RESPONSE:

_____

_____

_____

_____

_____

_____

_____

_____

_____

_____

_____

_____

_____

_____

_____

_____

_____

_____

_____

_____

_____

THE BIG RED LETTER

Let's make that big red letter an "S." For today's purpose, it will stand for shame. In 1850, Nathaniel Hawthorne wrote a book called *The Scarlet Letter*, which was about a woman who was caught in adultery. She was supposed to wear the red letter everywhere she went to expose her "wrongdoing." That was the thinking forever ago, and it was archaic. But what if you feel like you are wearing that big red letter currently?

Trauma and shame are connected but are bad buds. I am going to help you with that breakup in the skills below. Shame is a combination of emotions such as insecurity, humiliation, anger, embarrassment, worthlessness, powerlessness, hopelessness, helplessness, rejection, and inadequacy. There is also a feeling of being flawed, unloved, uncertain, and devalued. What heaviness that is to be carrying it around. They are all seriously negative. Humiliation is a tough one as it makes a person feel so low they could end up with depression, anxiety, post-traumatic stress, or even suicidal ideation. The person doing the humiliating is trying to exert power and purposefully embarrass the victim. Feeling ashamed will cause a person to struggle with self-esteem as well. In essence, guilt is about you making a mistake, and shame is about you being the mistake. That is not my opinion nor God's. Let's fix that.

The trauma connection is when something is done to us, such

as neglect/abuse, violence, rejection, being hated, or, as mentioned, being humiliated. Then, one will feel damaged and want to hide. The inward dialogue of painful feelings is, "I cannot let anyone know about this." That would cause rejection. The shame and trauma can also manifest due to dysfunctions such as your family having been incarcerated, having addictions, having certain medical or mental health conditions, their socio-economic status, their morals taking a nosedive, and concerns such as appearance, work circumstances, cultural aspects, marriage, etc.... Don't think there is less shame to those situations because they may not involve you personally, but there could be a feeling of shame if your family member is in prison for a crime, especially if it is heinous, someone can't keep a job, parents are going through, yet another divorce, or family is homeless. The person experiencing shame will most likely have experienced being rejected, criticized, and judged, and now there is a side of fear. You might even get stomach aches because it feels like "everyone is judging me." Trauma survivors should not blame themselves.

When a person is experiencing the negative emotions of shame, the brain acts like it is in danger. Thus, the sympathetic nervous system is activated, and a "fight, flight, freeze" response may result. The flight response triggers the feeling of needing to disappear. The fight response expresses itself as verbal and behavioral aggression by the embarrassed person towards the other who caused them to feel ashamed. The freeze response is what normally occurs when people are faced with trauma where they feel trapped and powerless. The freeze response allows a person to survive situations where intolerable things are happening to them.[3]

What does shame look like? A person may look down and avoid eye contact. Speech may be hesitant, and talk is most likely

---

3 Shirley Davis, *The Neuroscience of Shame.* (April 2019)

in a quieter voice. That person feeling shame may even clear their throat a few times. Posture may be slumped. Some people who are feeling shame may cover their face with their hands, fidget, pace, and offer a false smile. They might blush or bite their lips, tongue, or fingernails. Other times, that person might feel confused, and their mind might seem to go blank.

You may not recognize that there are ways you behave when feeling shame. Examine if any of these are true: you strike out at others, withdraw, refuse to talk to anyone about your feelings, blame others for how you feel, have unrealistic expectations for yourself, act defensively, are overly apologetic, and are a procrastinator. Shame likes to partner with guilt. The shame can be hidden, but bringing it out can be empowering and help to diffuse the power it has over you.

There is a connection between being a perfectionist and shame. Shame can turn a person into a perfectionist. That is because the perfectionist believes they have to do everything perfectly. That person tries very hard to avoid imperfection. They feel like they won't be loved if they don't do all things perfectly. What happened to that child who turned into a perfectionist and henceforth holds shame? Much of it is due to adverse childhood experiences. Possibly, the child was exposed to harsh criticism, neglect, or punishment that was inappropriate, which translated to not feeling deserving or enough. Somehow, the fear of failure latched on like a parasite, and thus, that child/adult had feelings of unworthiness.

Regarding trauma, if a child is abused, that child most likely will blame themselves for the actions of the one who has abused them. How sad and very erroneous. With such a negative event, they seek to gain some control as they fear being judged and thus experience disapproval from others. Perfectionists are driven to avoid failure. There is the constant feeling they are not good enough. It is quite a struggle.

Walt Disney Animation Studios did a movie called *Encanto*, released in 2021, where the main character, a teenager named Mirabel, suffers shame and judgment for being the only family member without a magical gift. It made her feel like she did not belong. She also tried to warn her family that their house was cracking, but they did not believe her. Her grandmother erroneously blamed her and looked down on her for not having a gift/magic. Mirabel thought she would never be good enough. There is a but to this story: Mirabel is able to bring the cracked house back to life again and restore relationships. Her shame turned to dignity and respect after she learned her gift was to bring healing.

Sometimes, people get angry at God due to the trauma they encounter. They expected God to intervene. He gets blamed and held responsible. When memories of traumatic events are quite harsh, the person's anger seems to seethe. Frustration latches on because of the hurt they believe God should have, could have, but didn't. Anger causes people to doubt His goodness and even His existence. Romans 8:6 reports that the mind controlled by the spirit is life and peace, and the sinful mind is hostile to God. Oh my, may it not be so to ever be hostile to the One who has such a deep love for us. Keep in mind that Satan is busy trying to steal, kill, and destroy, and we are the fallout of his schemes against us. The solution is to trust God's goodness and build faith. Divine providence will work in one's circumstance. Put down your angry fist at God and try telling God's enemy, Satan, "No." He will not have any hand in your heartache and to go to the abyss (bottomless pit). Resist him!

The Bible portrays the baby Jesus as born into a poor family in a lowly stable. As an infant, He was persecuted, causing His parents to have to move into hiding away from the death plans of King

Herod. When Jesus grew up, He was put to shame for doing miracles. He was rejected by His own people, as they picked the criminal Barabbas over Him to be freed. The Roman soldiers stripped Him, beat Him, mocked Him, and spat on Him. Isaiah 50:6 records that the Lord would endure His beard being plucked out. Note that pulling out the beard of a condemned man before crucifixion was part of the humiliation process. The Pharisees and scribes criticized Him. The Sanhedrin brought false charges against Him. He was handed over to be stoned because He declared He was God. People said He was mad and had a demon. The soldiers gambled for His bloodied clothes. When Jesus was on the cross, His disciple John, His mother, and two female friends were with Him; the other disciples fled. His humiliation spanned His entire life, as He suffered great scorn. He had the highest calling ever in history but had to deal with great hardship and extreme agony, especially the painful and shameful death on the cross. How did Jesus handle the whole shameful experience of His life and death? He bore it all on the cross, fulfilled His divine purpose, and went to glory, sitting at the right hand of Father God, and now He is interceding for us.

SKILLS TO TRY:

1. Support is quite effective for the trauma survivor. That is because the camaraderie from those who have been through a similar experience builds trust and understanding. It helps a person feel like they belong and reduces the shame.

2. Shame can grow; it has power, and it's destructive. With that, there could be damaging habits and negative feelings that grow with it, such as self-hatred. Self-compassion is needed big time. It includes being kind to yourself. Take care of your mind, body, and spirit.

3. Give up those self-critical thoughts. Being so hard on yourself will make you feel weaker. Failure is a common human experience, and I repeat, we all make mistakes. Apply a load of God's grace, mercy, and self-forgiveness. Accept that mistakes will be made your whole life, but move forward and learn from them. Try saying, "I made a mistake," but then give yourself some slack.

4. Sometimes, that critical voice repeats what has been said to you as a child. What did family, so-called friends, teachers, or neighbors say to you as a child that caused you to feel devalued? Were you told you are stupid, ugly, good for nothing, wish you were never born, etc.? A therapist would be helpful to overcome these negative statements that are most likely buried deep. Behind that negative evaluation could be depression and anxiety. Be patient with yourself.

5. You must never feel like damaged goods. Come out from your hiding place. Accept that there was a very negative event(s) and begin to fall into acceptance. It happened, and it is history. Now what? You are loved by God just as you are. There is work to be done, but it can be done.

6. There are memories that need healing. Feelings need to be faced. I am going to recommend a licensed mental health professional to help you deal with those memories and do so in a safe environment where you are under professional care. Quite possibly, with memories of trauma, you could have post-traumatic stress disorder, and a therapist can help with managing the symptoms while you go through the process of healing. It is a process with multiple layers, not a one-stop experience.

There are walls that need to come down. Be willing. Better days are ahead.

7. Have a dialogue with yourself of positive statements. Shame is irrational. Say these to yourself:

   A. My life has meaning and value.

   B. I have made mistakes, but I am not a mistake.

   C. Shame is temporary as I am making changes to overcome the shame.

   D. I will learn to accept, value, and love myself.

   E. The past does not define me in the present.

   F. I will choose to live my life one day at a time and be happy.

   G. I am enough.

   H. I believe in myself, my abilities, and my strengths.

   I. I can have healthy relationships.

   J. I will ask for help if and when I need it.

8. Self-esteem took a hit when shame entered. Tell yourself what you are good at, things you like about yourself, what your successes are, things that bring positive pride, and things you love to do. Remind yourself what brings you joy, and do more of those things.

9. Ask yourself if what is causing you shame is sensible or even accurate. Is it out of proportion in your mind? To counteract this, ask yourself if you have been jumping to conclusions as, after all, your life has been one hurdle after another. You will need to be very self-aware so you don't magnify the painful experiences in your mind.

10. Hold on and renew your faith in God, who is always for us. Whenever I have been in a hard place, I choose to press in closer to the Lord and trust His promises, no matter how long it takes for them to come to fruition. I look for His presence with me and that He has me. He really has me.

11. Practice gratitude. With that, you are expressing what is good. Trauma is all about the bad that happened, but moving forward, one must look to the things that help you find joy again. Gratitude will help diminish the negative history so you can focus on what is positive. Gratitude redirects your thinking away from suffering, and quite possibly, you can see some good things. When the next difficult event comes along, and it will because it is life, then that more grateful perspective will help to climb over its challenges. Start with writing down what you appreciate and are grateful for. Add to it daily. See if you can get to a hundred.

12. Make a list of the places where you want to make changes and begin to eliminate shame. For example, are there relationships you feel like you let down and want to restore? Do you want to improve your finances? Do you want to advance your educational status? Do you want to upgrade your housing? Do you want to polish up your appearance? Do you want to boost your attitude about things that seem like they can't change, such as a disability? Say why you feel shame and then how you will go about the changes.

13. For the perfectionist who is holding onto shame, allow yourself to do things imperfectly. I know that is a hard one. Don't let failures define you. Respect and love

yourself. Make your goals reasonable. Receive appropriate criticism, as you usually take it too personally. Stop beating yourself up. You procrastinate because you fear failure, so be realistic about what things need to be done, in what time frame, and by whom. Don't fixate on what may be negative about yourself. Find meaning in what you do, not that it must be done perfectly.

"Let us fix our eyes on Jesus, the author and perfector of our faith, who for the joy set before him endured the cross, scorning its shame, and sat down at the right hand of God" (Hebrews 12:2, BSB).

It's a call to keep on keeping on. One does that by fixing one's eyes on Jesus. How can we live out our faith without joy? The joy of the Lord is our strength. Jesus' joy was that He would be with Father God soon and forever. Crucifixion was a torturous, painful, and shameful way to be executed. But Jesus scorned shame by making it a means of salvation for us.

RESPONSE:

_____

_____

_____

_____

_____

_____

_____

_____

_____

_____

_____

_____

_____

_____

_____

_____

_____

_____

_____

_____

PREPOSTEROUS, DEPRAVED, AND TRAUMATIC

Here are some clues as to who was preposterous, depraved, and lived a life of trauma. She is a woman who portrayed the role of being rich, rude, spoiled, vain, greedy, entitled, and revengeful. She really had an evil, twisted personality. She cruelly drowned her own cat's kittens. She abused her own Persian cat, whom she freely admits she would have killed had it not been that the cat was worth a significant amount of money. She had murderous thoughts about killing dogs. The biggest clue is she is the lead actress in a famous old-time animated Disney movie involving dogs. Any guesses? Here is the answer: It's Cruella de Vil from *101 Dalmatians*. You know the story of her being infatuated with furs so much that she wanted all the Dalmatian puppies she could get for the purpose of killing the pups to use their hair for her furs.

But did you know what her trauma was? She witnessed her mother's murder and became an orphan. Her father was deceased. Apparently, the original movie and the remake, named *Cruella*, tell of her younger life in London.[4, 5] She was kicked out of school

---

4 Geronimi, Clyde, and Hamilton Luske. *One Hundred and One Dalmatians*. 1961. Burbank, CA: Walt Disney Productions.
5 Gillespie, Craig. *Cruella*. 2021. Burbank, CA: Walt Disney Pictures.

for beating up boys, and in trying to have a new start, her mother died by falling over a balcony. She feels like she has nowhere to turn, so she makes two friends who are thugs. She had a disorder called poliosis, which causes a decrease or absence of melatonin in the hair, which was the movie's explanation for her black and white hair. She has abandonment issues, grief, deception, revenge on her mind, and trauma and drama to the max. Can she be helped?

The Traumatic Stress Institute wrote an informative article called "Shame and Attachment,"[6] to which the following three paragraphs are derived. With shame, a person is very worried about how others perceive them. The person feels like others look at them with disgust. They feel exposed, real or imagined. It is basically "I am as I am seen." With the intensity of that painful emotion comes a self-protective anger/rage. The brain interprets shame as a crisis, and thus, the crisis response system in it gives shame power, and the flight-fight response activates. The flight response is the behavioral response of desiring to disappear, and the fight is the verbal and behavioral expression of blame and rage directed toward another. The more prone an individual is to feel shame, the more prone they will be to having self-esteem deficits, blaming others, holding onto resentments, and the less likely they are to feel empathy.

There is a direct relationship between shame-proneness and depression, suicide, anxiety, addictions, and family violence. Shame-proneness in grade school accurately predicts all the following in young adulthood: drug and alcohol use, risky sexual behavior, legal involvement, suicide attempts, and degree of involvement or no involvement with the community.

Although the two Cruella stories are just that, fiction and Dis-

---

6 Wilcox, P. (2010) *Shame and Attachment*, Traumatic Stress Institute. Available at: https://traumaticstressinstitute.org/wp-content/files_mf/1276631745ShameandAttachment.pdf (Accessed: 14 September 2023).

ney movies, they have a point. Cruella's shame-rage turned into revenge, which is often a real-life case. The shame-rage aims to triumph over and humiliate another so that the person is put in the position of experiencing shame.

My story of shame started at the early age of nine. My father sat us three children down and told us he was leaving us as he had found someone else. The message to me was, "You are not enough for me to stay." I had a wonderful mother and grandfather who saw to it that, in spite of family drama, I had a good upbringing. How did that fateful decision on my father's part play out? I became shy and didn't ask for much. I did not want to be a burden on my mom's finances, even though she never made me feel like I was. All my needs were met. I struggled with low self-esteem even though I did not know what that meant at the time. I never wanted my picture taken. That was me wanting to withdraw, which is a common response to shame. My mother got divorced, and when she signed my school reports, she signed with her maiden name. That made me feel odd and different not to have the same last name. We were the only family in the neighborhood that had that "stigma" of divorce. I did not have the maturity to handle it. Nowadays, it's so common that people would not think twice. Later in life, another issue of shame raised its ugly head when a family member's name appeared in the newspaper for something negative. That occasion caused embarrassment. Forgiveness became a work in progress. Depression began to creep in like a slick enemy, starting off minor and then increasing its grip over the years. There was also some shame from having to struggle financially for a significant amount of time with a paycheck that was not enough and occasionally late notices or threats of having utilities turned off.

For me, or the fictional Cruella, shame came from a self-evaluation of generally feeling bad and devalued. Hiding underneath is a fear of being judged, criticized, or rejected. The rejection part was there, and I had that feeling of "What will others think?" Insecurity attached to me like a tick. I could easily pick out my physical flaws. I can still easily do that.

"Choosing Therapy, Shame: Causes, Effects, and How to Overcome" lists the following common painful childhood experiences that may not be considered trauma but have similar lasting emotional impacts:

A. Being compared to a sibling and continuing to negatively compare yourself to them now.

B. Being scolded for making a mistake and internalizing the message that you are bad.

C. Making a mistake that resulted in someone else being hurt and not forgiving yourself.

D. Being bullied in school for how you looked or some other trait you became ashamed of.

E. Receiving love that felt conditional upon your performance in school/sports, etc..

F. Growing up in a house where it was shameful to show or talk about feelings.

G. Having a deeply guarded family secret you were expected to keep and protect.

H. Feeling ashamed of where or how you grew up, how much money you had, etc..

I. Having parents or caregivers who had unrealistic or perfectionistic expectations of you.

J. Being subject to frequent criticism, comparison, or disapproval.

K.   Having an absent parent and believing you were unloved.

So, I am all about solutions and coping with what life has
thrown at us. Take this saying in like a fresh breeze:

The most beautiful people we have known are those who have
known defeat, suffering, and loss and have found their way out of
the depths. These persons have an appreciation, sensitivity, and
understanding of life that fills them with compassion, gentleness,
and a deep, loving concern.

"Beautiful people do not just happen."

Elisabeth Kubler-Ross

Some of us feel like we fell into the cavern. Maybe some even
jumped over the dark cavern of grief and trauma. You could celebrate because you did it. Yes, gashed, bashed, and trashed through
some of life's negative events. They no doubt shaped us. Those
scars are reminders that it was difficult, but we overcame it. We
can be like the saying above: find a way, appreciate life, be sensitive and understanding, and respond to others with compassion,
gentleness, and loving concern.

There is something important to know about overcoming
shame. It's called God's grace. Many don't understand it. It is God
working in, through, and for us. It's His influence, care, and protection that gives us strength, endurance, help, favor, and compassion
for whatever is on our road. It is Him helping us bear up under it. It
is God giving us forgiveness and a new life as we allow the Lord to
change our minds and hearts. He gives us full acceptance. He takes
away one's shame. It is a free gift. It's yours; accept God's help.

SKILLS TO TRY:

1. Never lose sight of your strengths and abilities. List them. It will help you improve your quality of life, and that includes your mental health. You can discover what you are good at, which sets you up for success. Develop your strengths even more. We all need a moral boost when going through tough times. You will find yourself more engaged in positive things, and joy will take over the not-so-joyful days. Make an impact and feel good; you will stimulate the feel-good hormones. Show yourself some appreciation, and confidence will come on the scene.

2. Don't be so fast to make decisions. Can you slow down enough to avoid the choices that would lead to shame? For example, if you use alcohol to help you unwind or even escape, what happens to you after too many drinks? Shame would happen if you got obnoxious, embarrassed yourself, and all the other ramifications of excess use. When you choose to attend the party where Lucy Loose and Hanky Panky are also attending, and you have a weak moment, how will you feel if you cross the line of your own morals? Shame would probably eat you up.

3. Self-acceptance is a gift. Choose it wholeheartedly. Don't compare yourself to those more beautiful, more athletic, smarter, and those with better relationships and possessions. Don't compare your children with other children. Why? The shame connection is "they have, and I don't have." It can lead to self-rejection, self-depreciation, and depression. Your self-worth will take a hit, and you will feel less than. The shame of comparisons makes you feel not good enough. It

makes you feel that you missed the line that had "more" on it and got in the line that said "less" or "mediocre." Value yourself. Everybody is different and has very different circumstances. Life happened, both good and bad. You may live to be an old person—will you torture yourself with comparisons, or will you accept and love the unique you? Work with and make the best of what you have. Improve things as you can.

4. Fight for your tomorrow. That is for a healthy one. It helps if you stay in positive environments and with uplifting people. Take a look at both your environment and your connections. What needs to stay and be appreciated, and what do you need to eliminate? Live and give yourself chances to move forward. If you need some motivation to make goals and necessary changes, then part of your people need to be those who bring cheers, encouragement, and hope and are wise and discerning.

5. Watch what you say to yourself. As mentioned before and worthy of a repeat: how do you think you will stomp out shame if you agree with your negative voice that tells you, "You deserve to be punished" or "You are a bad seed"? Since the inner critic is normally powerful and sets out to defame you, you will need to disarm it. Some give it a name to say no to, of whatever choosing you like, such as Blake Blubbering or Eric Erroneous, and some may choose to use a scripture such as in Matthew 16:23a (NIV), "Jesus turned and said to Peter, Get behind me Satan." After all, Satan is behind all the ways to see to your demise, so tell him off.

6. Spiritually speaking, guilt can be constructive, but shame is always destructive. Consider allowing the Lord to help with

the managing of that. He has that grace, as just mentioned above. He gives us everything we need to live a life of victory. Come to him with your load of guilt, shame, regrets, bad decisions, and hurt you have and hurt you caused. Not you or anyone else you know is perfect. Things will be out of your control sometimes, but God can help you find a safe place, balanced with self-love and acceptance of His love, to help you on the path He designed. It's a journey, the process of getting there, becoming more Christ-like, and bringing His kind of healing, which includes a peace like none other.

"My soul is weary with sorrow; strengthen me according to your word. Keep me from deceitful ways; be gracious to me through your law. I have chosen the way of truth; I have set my heart on your laws. I hold fast to your statutes, O Lord, do not let me be put to shame" (Psalm 119:28–31, NIV).

This is a person who is overwhelmed and asking that God strengthen them with the words of truth from God. This person believes that God is able to keep him from deceitful ways and will pour grace into his life and circumstances. He also asks that since he has chosen to hold onto God's words, God will not let him be ashamed. It sounds like faith and hope. It's a great idea.

RESPONSE:

THE WHOLE TOWN MOURNED

The title sounds like something terrible happened, like an earthquake, tsunami, flood, hurricane, shooting, or fire that went through the town. It does involve many deaths. It's the story of a massacre ordered by Herod the Great from the Bible (Matthew 2:1–18). Herod was called "The Great" because of the mammoth size structures he ordered built. He was anything but great due to his ruthless dealings with his family and his kingdom. He had ordered the killing of three of his own sons, his wife, three elders, and forty-six members of the Sanhedrin. His character was tyrannical, very paranoid, and cold-blooded. He seemed to be deranged. As the story goes, when he heard of a baby boy (Jesus) who was being called "King of the Jews," he sent the Magi to find Him under the guise he wanted to go and worship Him. This was the opposite of King Herod's plan, as he was prone to kill anyone who was a threat to his throne. The Magi found the Christ child, and they were warned by the Lord not to return to Herod. The result was the king ordered the massacre of baby boys under the age of two years old. It was sadly one of very great wailing and mourning.

That event was called "The Massacre of the Innocent." If you witness a murder or are affected by the murder of others, you will have trouble getting that picture out of your head. It could be considered that the whole town had post-traumatic stress or even complicated post-traumatic stress. There would be secondary trauma. I will not give any descriptions of what they were spectators of. But those who witnessed or were intimately involved as family and friends can attest to the visual that can haunt a person. They would have seen those babies' faces daily. The family and onlookers had to go face to face with the aftermath: the visuals, the screams, the flashbacks, and the nightmares. There is a suffering that a person has to wrestle with, a loss that goes so deep. There is a part where an individual cannot make sense of it, and it seems to include spiritually questioning God. God gets blamed. God seems to be blamed as people, being human, are very hurt and overwhelmed. They also feel helpless and feel out of control. Tragedies are personal and devastating. I expect since He made us with human emotions, He understands.

To blame God means He made a mistake. He rules, reigns, and runs the universe, and there are no mistakes with Him. I most highly suggest that instead of telling God that He must have slipped up, go to Him for His special kind of comfort that is like none other. Job did not charge God with wrongdoing. There was definitely some serious wrong happening to Job (Job 1:22). It is quite amazing that Job was able to say, "Though He slay me, yet will I hope in Him" (Job 13:15, NIV). We do not sit in the heavens and get to make decisions on who gets the short end of the stick and who doesn't. Being a good person does not stop bad things from happening. He has higher purposes that our minds and hearts do not comprehend. Asking for God's will in all our scenarios sets in motion His greater purpose.

Dr. Matthew Stanford wrote an article called "Five Things the Scripture Teach Us about Trauma and Suffering."[7] Glean from the

---

7 Stanford, Dr. Matthew. *"Five Things the Scriptures Teach Us about Trauma and Suffering."* Hope and Healing Center and Institute, November 23, 2021. https://hopeandhealingcenter.org/five-things-the-scriptures-teach-us-about-trauma-and-suffering-by-dr-matthew-s-stanford/.

wisdom of his article.

1. ***God is present and in control of our suffering.*** From our limited perspective, pain and suffering seem contrary to our idea of a sovereign God who is good and loving. We forget that Adam chose to sin, and we live in a fallen world full of suffering. Suffering should not cause us to question God's sovereignty. God is sovereign despite our circumstances. He created all things, and He is in control of all things.

2. ***That God is good and cares for us.*** We have all heard this statement: "How could a loving God allow_____?" The Creator of the World made a way for disobedient, powerless creatures to come into an eternal relationship with Him. He is patient and gracious. He became one of us and then sacrificed Himself for us. Self-sacrifice is the ultimate act of love.

3. ***Through our trials and suffering, we have an opportunity to draw closer to God.*** Even Jesus was sad when He went through difficult times at Lazarus's grave, in the garden of Gethsemane, and on the cross. Through our trials and suffering, we have an opportunity to draw closer to God. During the easy times, we often become self-reliant, forgetting our need for God. It is in the hard times, when our faith is tested, that we recognize our need for complete dependence on Him. Persevering through difficult times develops a mature and complete faith. We are ever being conformed to the image of Christ, and suffering is a necessary part of that transformation.

4. ***Jesus understands what it is to suffer.*** We do not worship a distant, unapproachable God. We worship a God

that knows what it is to be human and to suffer. His whole life was full of suffering. He was born into poverty in a country occupied by a cruel army. He narrowly escaped a mass slaughtering of children that was ordered because of His birth. He was physically assaulted (I would use the word challenged) by Satan, persecuted because of His teaching, thought insane by His family, betrayed by His own disciples, deserted by His friends, falsely accused, publicly humiliated, beaten to the point of death, and then slowly, painfully and publicly executed by crucifixion as a common criminal.

5. ***Our identity is grounded in Christ.*** Our identity is not defined by traumatic events or suffering but is grounded in Christ. God does not see you as a victim. He sees you as His child. The scriptures tell us that as children of God, we were chosen before the creation of the world to be holy and blameless adopted sons and daughters, lavished with understanding and marked with the Holy Spirit. We must not allow tragedy or circumstances to define who we are or how we live. We have His very life within us, and we choose to live out that truth.

God does not waste the events that happen to us. He can use what has happened in His way and time. Evil is present in the world, but balance that out with knowing God's presence is with us, and we win over the evil. His presence is sufficient to meet our challenges. One's past is in His hands, and so is one's future.

In case you are wondering how God can heal a person from post-traumatic stress disorder, consider these points from Honey Lake Clinic:[8]

---

8 Honey Lake. "How God Heals PTSD." Honey Lake, November 13, 2017. https://www.honeylake.clinic/blog/how-god-heals-ptsd/.

1. He heals with the hope of eternal peace.

2. Soothing emotions, distress, and worries through prayer.

3. Peace knowing that our past and future are in God's hands.

4. Forgiveness by taking Jesus' example and forgiving the cause of the trauma and releasing that burden.

5. Answers by finding out why we are hurt, what our purpose and value in life are, and why we are here.

6. Security in knowing that you can overcome adversity from trauma and have the resources to cope just as Jesus, David, Peter, Paul, and Stephen did.

7. Acceptance that not everything is in our control or going to go the way that we planned but in His plan.

8. Grace because even though we make many mistakes and shame turn us away from Him, He still gives us a chance to be and feel at peace with Him.

9. Power as God gives us a supernatural strength to overcome our many obstacles and become closer to Him in our darkest times.

10. Unconditional love that He will always have us no matter how many mistakes we make.

11. Relief when Jesus takes away our burdens from us.

SKILLS TO TRY:

1. Read the first five points and take them in like smelling a beautiful flower, even though nothing or very little smells beautiful in your life. Find something lovely to smell to activate the smell gland. Certain smells lower stress levels and improve your mood.

2. Go over the next set of eleven nuggets and process them emotionally so you can build up your faith and realize that God is in your heartache.

3. Go to God in prayer and tell Him how you feel. It might include anger, confusion, and great hurt. If all you can say is "help," then so be it. God will get it. At least you brought it to Him.

4. If you are with someone who is having a flashback, tell them that they are having a flashback and encourage them to breathe slowly and deeply. Do this with that person if possible. Be aware that they may not be able to connect with reality. Do not touch them, but when they come out of it, ask if they want to be touched. Don't be offended if that response is a no. Don't make any sudden movements. The person having the flashback will be overwhelmed. They will likely feel helpless and confused. Help them return to the present by saying something like, "Bert, this is your best friend, Al. You are here with me at my house, and you are safe." Encourage them to open their eyes and see they are in the present and safe. Repeat again that they are safe with you and not where they will get hurt.

5. If you are having a flashback and happen to realize it, then tell yourself, "This is a flashback; the trauma

is over, and I survived. I am safe." Remind yourself you are in the present. Use your senses of sight, hearing, smell, touch, and taste. Move into another area or room. Talk to a trusted person.

6. Make sure to take slow, deep breaths. It will help you increase your oxygen so you can move out of anxiety and lessen the possibility that you will panic.

7. Find what makes you feel safe and secure. Is it hugging your pet, wrapping up in a blanket, or being alone or not alone in a room?

8. Learning what the trigger for the flashback is will help you feel more in control, and you can problem-solve by analyzing what happened before and what you heard and felt. For example, if the noise from construction on a certain street triggers you, then you can go through a different route.

9. It is recommended to see a mental health professional for an evaluation. Many survivors of trauma get prescribed an antidepressant and anti-anxiety medication. Getting help using cognitive behavioral therapy has proven to be beneficial in helping you change your thinking about the trauma so you are less stressed.

"But as for me, I watch in hope for the Lord, I wait for God my savior; my God will hear me. Do not gloat over me, my enemy! Though I have fallen, I will rise. Though I sit in darkness, the Lord will be my light" (Micah 7:7–8, NIV).

Falling refers to calamity, and darkness means distress or misery. Yet, with all that going on, the author, Micah (a prophet), is looking for hope, waiting, and believing he is heard. There is a confidence that says, "I will rise." Yes, get up, don't stay down!

There is trust that is needed, knowing that the Lord will deliver in His time. Look for Him and look to Him.

RESPONSE:

_____

_____

_____

_____

_____

_____

_____

_____

_____

_____

_____

_____

_____

_____

_____

_____

_____

_____

_____

_____

_____

_____

A MOAT COULD
BE NEEDED

A moat, you say? It is a body of water around a castle or town to keep people out. Mostly, it was used back in the day to protect the inhabitants from attack. It might have water, or it might be dry as in a ditch. If it was back in medieval times, then there was quite an amount of violence, and it was very much needed. Moats have strong walls. That is a clue. We need strong walls—that's our exterior. We also need strength for our hearts.

Pretend a moat is a boundary as it is. Whether you have or have not survived a trauma, everybody needs a boundary. Actually, that would be boundaries—several of them. A boundary is, in its simplest form, a dividing line. It shows where an area begins and another ends. For relationships, boundaries are needed. It tells others where you draw the line. It tells others what you are and are not comfortable with in a relationship or even in an activity. For instance, even if I won a bungee jumping prize, it would be a solid boundary of "it's not happening." A boundary lets people know what you need, value, and feel and what you don't want, need, and how you feel.

There are boundaries you need to set up physically, emotionally, sexually, intellectually, financially, spiritually, materially, and for time management. There are the non-negotiable ones I will call "No way Hosea boundaries." Remember, you have likely been hurt, so these are important limits that need to be set up for your well-being and to move forward. It will require that you tell others what your boundaries are and, if they are crossed, then what the consequences would be. I believe some of you may have trouble with telling others of the consequences. Possibly, that is because this is all too much. You have never done this before as you have let people walk all over you; they were violent or threatening, and you were afraid. Be careful! Have others with you for protection and strength. Some people are just heavily burdened, and it's another thing to do, and some people have trouble saying no.

Maybe people don't respect the boundaries you set because they haven't been there in the past. They have violated them to hurt you on purpose, they like the control they can have over you, or they just want to see "what you are gonna do about it." Here is an example: if Alfred Alkie seemed to get angry with you while he was inebriated or Wally Wanton seemed to have a wandering hand with you, then a boundary needs to be set. You also have the ability to problem solve whether to be near them as well. Beverly Belittling would be one I would set a boundary with where she could not be in my close circle of friends or maybe even be a friend at all.

Assertiveness is needed, especially with the Alfred Alkies or Wally Wantons of the world. That means you speak up for yourself without aggression. You speak up for your rights without violating anyone else's rights. In other words, you are not being passive and not being aggressive. Doing this can even decrease anxiety and depression, and by doing so, you decrease stress. Watch your self-esteem increase when you set up those parameters.

Of those boundaries mentioned in the previous paragraph, here are some definitions to help you at least know what you should be trying to set up.

Physical boundary: This is your personal space, your privacy, and your body. This boundary is to keep you safe. An example is when you say whether you are comfortable or not with public displays of affection. You will put in his or her place the person who is getting too close with ulterior motives or expecting touch or more when you don't. You call the shots as to how much privacy is needed. You get to tell someone if it is too late or too early to come over. Remember, it is your home, your space. You get to say no if you are resting and no if you need to eat or have other activities to take care of. For example, you need to say, "No, I don't want you to pinch me ever again."

Emotional boundary: This is about your feelings. You decide with whom and when you are comfortable sharing your feelings. You should not allow your feelings to be criticized, as that is disrespectful. You are not responsible for how other people feel, and they may try to make their own anger issues your fault. Setting up an emotional boundary helps a person say they will not answer questions that are inappropriate. Be careful not to share inappropriate information with your children. An example is, "I don't want to talk about my weight, age, or previous partners."

Sexual boundary: If you don't want someone to make sexual comments to you or touch you when it is not welcome, then you have a right to put that person in their place. You determine the if, when, where, how, frequency, and with whom. Discussing contraception and protecting one another's privacy is a sign of a healthy boundary. Nowadays, you may want to get your partner's sexual history, which may or may not include sexually transmitted diseases. A violation would be pressure to have sex, lying about anything sexual, unwanted sexual comments, punishing someone if they don't want to engage in sex, and unwanted touch or assault. A good boundary would be a positive conversation such as, "Are you comfortable with such and such?"

Intellectual boundary: This is about your thoughts and beliefs. You can let someone know if they monopolized conversations or shut you out of the conversation. Let someone know if they dis-missed you or belittled you. You can tell a person if their conver-sation is inappropriate or if you are offended, such as in racism. It's called having respect. My boundary would be, "I will not allow you to talk to me like that even if you don't share my opinion."

Financial boundary: You have a right to say no to lending to an irresponsible person who you know will not be paying you back. You also have a right to get paid for the service/work completed. You have a right to say no to joint bank accounts or how money should be divided and to set up a budget and adhere to it. Financial goals can be set up and whether or not your partner agrees to that. Money issues cause great stress, and setting a good boundary will prevent sorrow down the road. Many families struggle as the par-ents still have to financially help their adult children and vice ver-sa, adult children need to help their parents. Making it clear keeps resentment at bay. A boundary needs to be set as to whether or not to lend or just gift. Setting a financial boundary will also keep you on track from overspending. For example: "I said I wanted to save for a down payment on our house, so we agreed on a certain amount, and you are not following that agreement due to what you spend on eating out. Let's fix this."

Spiritual boundary: You get to believe in what you want, to wor-ship the way you want or not, and to practice your religion as you want. You do not have to be manipulated into going to any religious meetings unless you choose to. However, due to the many different religions nowadays, start with something you at least know to be true or that you can be certain that God was with you at such and such a time. Maybe a truth was "For God so loved the world that He gave His one and only Son that whoever believes in Him shall not perish but have everlasting life." (John 3:16, NIV). I grew up with the song "Jesus Loves Me This I Know for the Bible Tells Me So." It is very solidly an unwavering fact for me.

Material boundary: Refers to your possession and money. You may allow things to be borrowed, such as your car, lawnmower, jewelry, clothes, money, etc. You can say no if you want to. You need to inform any person borrowing from you how you expect it to be returned. This will help you not feel resentful if you lent your car yet again when there was plenty of gas and it got returned near empty. An example would be, "I lent you money last month with your promise you would return it promptly after your payday, but you did not, so at this time, it is a no."

Time boundary: This protects how you spend your time and from doing activities you do not want to do. You have a right not to have people waste your time, and you do not have to volunteer if you do not want to. You will want to understand your priorities and be sure you have allowed time for you and what you want. It's not selfish. It helps you to not overcommit. An example would be, "I can help you on Saturday, but not until after 2:00 p.m." My thing that friends and family don't always understand is I like shorter meetings, visits, and phone calls rather than longer. There are exceptions, of course.

Non-negotiable boundary: This is a deal breaker. These include things like there will be no relationship with you if you are cheating on me, abusing me emotionally or physically, using drugs or excessively drinking, treating me, my children, grandchildren, or pets wrong, driving with you if it is risky, or doing anything that makes me not feel safe.

God set boundaries up for us so we would not get caught up in the snares of the enemy, and we would take the higher ground. It also gives us good direction so we don't go the wrong way. It is good self-care.

Did you ever wonder if Jesus set up boundaries? In Bill Gaultiere's book *Your Best Life in Jesus' Easy Yoke: Rhythms of Grace to De-Stress and Live Empowered*[9], there are some examples listed of how Jesus set up boundaries:

He accepted His personal limits:

1.   He enjoyed solitude. He withdrew from the crowds to

---

9 Gaultiere, Bill. *Your Best Life In Jesus' Easy Yoke: Rhythms of Grace to De-Stress and Live Empowered.* CreateSpace Independent Publishing Platform, 2016

go away on retreats, alone or with friends.

2. He enjoyed the moment (these people, this place, this time). He could not be in two places at the same time (Mark 1:38).

3. Jesus had an unhurried pace of life. He was never in a hurry except to go to Jerusalem and embrace His cross (John 11:6; Mark 10:32).

Jesus also said no to inappropriate behavior:

4. Demands: He withdrew from the crowds who wanted Him for one-on-one time with the Father (Luke 5:15–16).

5. Entitlement: He didn't give in to His mother and brothers, who tried to use their relationship with Him to pull Him away from the crowd he was ministering to (Matthew 12: 46–50).

6. Cynicism: Jesus said no to Herod's mocking demand, "Show us a sign that you are the son of God." (Luke 23:8–9).

7. Manipulation: He said no to Peter and the disciples, who had an inappropriate agenda for Jesus to be a political king or military leader rather than a sacrificial lamb (Matthew 16:58).

Jesus spoke the truth in Love to those stuck or wrong:

8. Exploitation: He used a whip to clear out the temple of the vendors and money changers who were taking advantage of the poor and turning God's house into a marketplace (Matthew 21:12–17; John 2:12–16).

9. Misguided: Jesus rebuked the disciples who tried to

keep the little children away from Him and told them they needed to emulate the children's faith (Matthew 19:13–15).

Jesus had expectations for people in need:

10. "What do you want?": Two blind men called out to Him for help from the Jericho Road. He asked them, "What do you want?" They needed to ask for what they needed, and they needed to trust Him (Matthew 20:29–34).

11. "Do you want to get well?": For thirty-eight years, the invalid at the Sheep Gate pool hadn't been able to get into the miracle waters. He felt hopeless and sorry for himself. Jesus challenged him, "Do you want to get well?… Get up! Pick up your mat and walk." It was up to that person to be motivated and take responsibility for himself (John 5:1–14).

Jesus offered grace and truth according to the need (John 8:1–11):

12. The humble and broken: To the woman caught in adultery, he offered grace ("Neither do I condemn you") and truth ("Go and sin no more").

13. The proud and self-righteous: To the Pharisees who tried to condemn this woman and to trap Jesus, He listened (grace) and then confronted their pride and scapegoating with the truth ("Let him who is without sin throw the first stone").

If you have been involved in any traumatic experience, then I can expect that you were with aggressive, toxic, or inappropriate people who somehow disrespected you. I hate that for you. But let's just take a look at how to not be with those people or to set better boundaries if you choose to keep the relationship. Maybe it's education, so you don't get caught in that scenario again.

Identify who makes you feel bad after having time with them. Have you identified the people who use you and manipulate you? Do you feel the life drains out of you after you have had time with them? Are they full of drama and suck you into it? Do they give you anxiety? Do they talk at you and not with you? Are you told you are wrong a lot? Are you criticized and put down, along with your family and friends being put down? Do they make you feel insecure? Do you feel like you are even seen? Are you on the receiving end of their frequent anger? Do they make you feel you are always doing the wrong thing? Are they whittling away at your self-esteem? Are you constantly questioned as to what you did with your money, who you were with, why you were late, or actually a bunch of whys, where, and how comes? Do they play mind games with you? Do you feel trapped? Are the boundaries you set up ever respected? If you are not safe, then get reinforcements and get safe! You know, down deep inside, that person cannot be trusted.

SKILLS TO TRY TO SET BOUNDARIES:

1. Identify where you need a moat/boundary. I have listed eight and a non-negotiable from paragraph 3. Make your list.

2. From the examples where Jesus set up boundaries, do you see where you can include any of those?

3. From the above paragraph, sixteen questions were asked. Answer and see what is needed as a plan of action. I expect this was eye-opening.

4. See if you have lost self-respect. That is a true sign you need a moat. I mean, you likely were invaded. Do you

really want the best version of yourself in your castle? Do you feel proud of yourself? Okay, not so much? Then, go back to your values. Are they being violated? Did your self-worth get flushed away? Maybe to be respected and loved, you became a people pleaser. Your castle exterior and interior will crack with all that negativity and neglect. Are you tolerating abuse? No, no, no, you do not deserve that!

5. Start with you from the beginning—build a strong wall. Write ways you will love and respect yourself and then put them into action.

6. Well-set boundaries protect your mental well-being. My suggestion is to start with just a few boundaries. Get the safety ones in place, and then the next one that is most important to you. Be sure to stand up for yourself.

7. Be consistent. If your boundary is "We will not swear in front of the kids" or "We will not fight in front of the kids," and then you allow it a few times, you will not have things under control, and lines will be crossed. Confusion is created.

8. Communicate. If someone is regularly violating your boundaries, then have a chat about it. For instance, my family and friends know I go to bed at about 9:00 p.m., and my cell phone gets shut off at that time. I get up early, so they have all day to call me. I will always be available for emergencies. Communication is set for everyone to know where they stand. I also make sure to call family and friends before possibly visiting. If you didn't communicate it, then how can you enforce it?

9. Don't hold any guilt that you are changing things up a bit. Remember, it will improve your emotional health, improve your relationships, and set you up on a path of self-respect. Guilt means you did something wrong or didn't do what should have been done, but setting boundaries is the right thing.

10. Make sure your values are not violated and you understand your limitations. For instance, I showed up to work on time and did self-care by leaving on time. The job could often be very tiring to my mind, so I tried to take nothing home and helped my brain not be so drained. List where this may need to be tweaked.

"A hot-tempered man must pay the penalty; if you rescue him, you will have to do it again" (Proverbs 19:19, NIV).

If you allow a hot-tempered man to be in charge or be rescued, and you make excuses for him and allow it to continue (poor boundary lines), then you will only have to do it again. That man or woman does not learn, and they need to face consequences. Of course, run these matters by the Lord for wisdom.

RESPONSE:

_____

_____

_____

_____

_____

_____

_____

_____

_____

_____

_____

_____

_____

_____

_____

_____

_____

_____

_____

_____

_____

YOUR BEST
CALENDAR OF NOS

If you can say no when it is necessary and important to do so, then you are benefitting your mental health. It is important to value yourself, to prioritize yourself, and to set boundaries. If you need to and want to say no, it shows you can be in control; you get to decide who or what your priority is. It feels wonderful not to have someone try to control you. It also shows others that you value your time and priorities. Saying no when you need to will prevent burnout. Saying no is great self-care because it will help you prioritize your well-being. You will most likely feel like you can breathe easier and have energy and time for yourself and your family.

Here is your calendar of suggestions of things that are important to say "no" to or things to not do.

Day 1: Say no to any form of abuse.

Day 2: Say no to toxic relationships.

Day 3: Do not give your power away. If you have, take it back.

Day 4: Do not feel sorry for yourself.

Day 5: Do not say yes when you want or need to say no.

Day 6: Do not focus on things you can't control.

Day 7: Do not give up.

Day 8: Do not be a people-pleaser.

Day 9: Do not resent other people's success.

Day 10: Say no to negative thinking/talk.

Day 11: Say no to procrastination.

Day 12: Say no to fear.

Day 13: Say no to complaining and whining.

Day 14: Say no to gossip.

Day 15: Say no to eating the wrong foods.

Day 16: Say no to people, places, and things that drain your energy and resources.

Day 17: Say no to ungratefulness.

Day 18: Say no to perfectionism.

Day 19: Say no to bad habits.

Day 20: Say no to regrets. Accept your past.

Day 21: Say no to people who are takers.

Day 22: Say no to being overly sensitive.

Day 23: Say no to complacency.

Day 24: Say no to not setting boundaries.

Day 25: Say no to disrespectful language.

Day 26: Say no to unfairness/unkindness.

Day 27: Say no to chaos in your life.

Day 28: Say no to negative addictions.

Day 29: Say no to time wasters.

Day 30: Say no to lack of exercise.

Day 31: Say no to the devil and to everything he wants to steal from you.

SKILL TO TRY:

1. Go over each day and write down on your response page what you want to work on and how you will accomplish it. Do you need help/helpers? To break some negative habits, learning to set boundaries or eliminate chaos may require support from others. It may be helpful to have someone help with accountability to point out to you if you are letting people run over you, you are responding with anger, or you are in a negative thinking rut.

"And do not give the devil a foothold" (Ephesians 4:27, NIV).

The devil is an opportunist, looking for ways to get a hold of one's life. Do not give the evil one an opportunity to influence or infiltrate into your life. Life is full of enough havoc and distress. Don't allow things to enter or remain, as it is essentially giving Satan an invite in. May it not be so!

RESPONSE:

_____

_____

_____

_____

_____

_____

_____

_____

_____

_____

_____

_____

_____

_____

_____

_____

_____

_____

_____

_____

_____

_____

_____

_____

YOUR BEST CALENDAR YET

Yes, really, it can be your best year. Here is a month of "dos" for your self-care. Self-care helps you live your best life—that includes mental health and physical health. For this time being, it will include relationships as well. We feel good about ourselves when our relationships bring us some enjoyment and satisfaction. When we take care of ourselves, our stress levels go down, and our energy level goes up. Our health thus improves. Anxiety and depression are improved. Self-care improves our self-esteem. A person feels more empowered and utilizes their resiliency skills. Self-care helps you be mindful of your needs.

Here are suggestions for your daily calendar of self-care:

Day 1: Commit to your decision to make a change.

Day 2: Let your heart come alive to possibilities.

Day 3: Choose to be open-minded today.

Day 4: Tell yourself, "You will not obsess over anything."

Day 5: Give yourself a talk of "atta boy or atta girl."

Day 6: Choose to smile for yourself and at somebody else.

Day 7: Give up any resentment, bitterness, or hate.

Day 8: Learn something new every day.

Day 9: Give yourself a compliment and then give someone else a sincere one.

Day 10: Learn from someone else who has your best interest at heart.

Day 11: Be humble (not thinking you are better than others).

Day 12: Do an act of kindness for someone.

Day 13: Express your gratitude for something.

Day 14: List a handful of your strengths. Can you list more?

Day 15: Express praise to God.

Day 16: Express thanks to God.

Day 17: Start praying or increase your prayer time.

Day 18: Read your Bible regularly.

Day 19: Do not compare yourself to anyone else.

Day 20: Do something you used to enjoy but stopped doing.

Day 21: Call a friend to check on that person. Be a friend to them.

Day 22: Buy yourself a gift/treat, food, clothes, trinket, jewelry, etc.. A brownie is my go-to.

Day 23: Volunteer to do something for someone. Maybe

mow their grass, walk their dog, look at their car need, give a ride, bring them takeout, or help at a needed service organization.

Day 24: Invite someone over for tea, coffee, cookie, hamburger, or to chat.

Day 25: Do something to improve your environment.

Day 26: Spend time in nature.

Day 27: Consider being part of a spiritual community to grow and give.

Day 28: Do something fun, including laughter, singing, or dancing.

Day 29: Practice forgiveness.

Day 30: Hug yourself, someone you care about, or your pet. If you don't have anyone or a pet, then hug a stuffed animal or a pillow.

Day 31: Make sure you are in safe housing.

SKILLS TO TRY:

1. Read your one month's worth of "to-do" self-care suggestions. What needs tweaking? What can you incorporate?

2. Try making another whole month of creative and practical things to try to add to your care and, ultimately, your move towards a happier you.

"For we are God's workmanship, created in Christ Jesus to do good works, which God prepared in advance for us to do" (Ephesians 2:10, NIV).

The body of believers is His workmanship, so He looks at us as His very special handiwork. We are created with a purpose. That's His purpose for our lives. Since God created us so marvelously, we should treat ourselves with great care and love. We should discover what that unique plan is and then work to do it, all the while taking care of what He said was His remarkable craftmanship: you.

RESPONSE:

_____

_____

_____

_____

_____

_____

_____

_____

_____

_____

_____

_____

_____

_____

_____

_____

_____

_____

_____

_____

_____

_____

_____

ALPHABET SELF LOVE

*"An empty lantern provides no light. Self-care is the
fuel that allows your light to shine brightly."*

Unknown

*"True self-love is not bath salts and chocolate cake,
it's making the choice to build a life you don't need
to escape from."*

Brianna Wiest

*"Life tried to crush her, but only succeeded in creat-
ing a diamond."*

John Mark Green

*"I love the person I've become because I fought to
become her."*

Kaci Diane

*"Shout out to the people who haven't felt okay, but
are getting up every day and refusing to quit.
Stay strong."*

Unknown

Taking care of yourself and loving yourself are of high importance. To be at your top mental health and be the best version of

yourself requires you to do right by yourself. If you do the skills below, you will gain insight, and happiness will not evade you. I have gone through the alphabet with a skill for every letter of the alphabet:

A. Appreciate yourself. We are all flawed human beings, but you deserve love and good things.

B. Be your own best friend. Don't we love and value our best friends so much?

C. Communicate your needs to others. Realize your needs and wants. Be assertive.

D. Don't get validation from others. It could cause you to be a people pleaser. Validate yourself.

E. Empathy is what you should show yourself. Be gentle and kind with your feelings.

F. Forgive yourself for your past mistakes. There is power in it, and it decreases depression.

G. Gratitude is a positive expression and has good mental health benefits.

H. Have positive, supportive people in your life who value you and enjoy your company.

I. Improve your body image. It helps with better physical and mental health.

J. Joy needs to be created. The joy of the Lord is your strength. Don't neglect the spiritual.

K. Kindness is infectious. Give it out. It improves your mood and increases your self-esteem.

L. Liberate. Set yourself free from everything that has held you back.

M. Move it. That means exercise. It will lower your body's stress hormones.

N. "No" means "no"—sexually, physically, emotionally, and mentally. This shows self-respect.

O. Optimism. That means being hopeful and confident about the future.

P. Patience. You may have been years not taking care of yourself. Try a little at a time.

Q. Quit condemning yourself. It will make you feel worthless and likely depressed and anxious.

R. Respect yourself. Be proud of yourself and accept your imperfections. Be authentic.

S. Stand up for yourself and for what matters to you. Look out for your well-being.

T. Take vitamins and medications if prescribed. Be consistent. Accept that you may need them.

U. Unhealthy relationships need to go. They undermine your values, needs, and ideals.

V. Violence should not be tolerated in any way. Protect yourself.

W. Watch out for relationships that smother you, isolate you, take from you, and hurt you.

X. Xyst (a patio or garden walk). Try time in nature, in the sun or the water. Refresh yourself.

Y.   You can accept praise and compliments. Believe in yourself. Your self-esteem can be built up.

Z.   Zeal for life. It includes being strong, energetic, and passionate about a purpose.

SKILLS TO TRY:

1.   1. Take each one of the skills going through the alphabet and see where you are with each. Try some every day, practice them, and make the changes towards your life of wholeness. These are not "fixes." They are "helps" for your journey.

2.   2. You may find it interesting to see if you can go through the alphabet yourself with some further skills or ideas to try. Think outside of the box as well as think simple. For example: "F" can be a foot soak, "M" can be a mask for your face, "R" can be a ride, "G" can be for going to a farmer's market, "S" can be going on a swing and "T" can be a treat for you. It's your list and your way. Just add good things.

"Do to others as you would have them do to you" (Luke 6:31, NIV).

This is what Jesus said in the Sermon on the Mount. It has been called the Golden Rule. Essentially, one should show kindness, concern, or help like you would want it shown to you. The Mosaic Law parallels this comment: "Whatever is hurtful to you, do not do that to another."

RESPONSE:

_____

_____

_____

_____

_____

_____

_____

_____

_____

_____

_____

_____

_____

_____

_____

_____

_____

_____

_____

_____

_____

_____

THE LEECH AND SELF-CARE

This is in reference to giving oneself some charity, which can be expanded to mean self-love, compassion, clemency, benevolence, goodwill, mercy, grace, and leniency. All those words are so good, and we should show them to ourselves. I am including this because those who struggle with depression and anxiety and have experienced trauma may need to take a look at themselves and see if they have been treating themselves with harsh criticism, poor self-regard, shame, self-hate, doubt, or sorrow. Those things hang on like a leech. That bloodsucker is really a parasitic worm that attaches as much as hurt and negative self-evaluation does. The leech has a pain killer in it, so when it breaks the skin, you don't feel it at first. It can suck five times its body weight in blood, and it can carry a disease. The disease, I will call it "The bad way you feel about yourself," the loss of blood is what is drained from you. That leech has three jaws, so when it bites a person, the jaws move in a sawing motion to open a wound. That is like not forgiving yourself, your history of criticizing yourself that saws through your life when you are trying to move forward.

The leech must be dislodged! Dislodge, according to the Oxford Dictionary,[10] means to remove from a position of power or au-

---

10 "Dislodge." Definition, pictures, pronunciation and usage notes | Oxford Advanced Learner's Dictionary at OxfordLearnersDictionaries.com. Accessed September 14, 2023. https://www.oxford-

thority. That is a great description of what you need to do with any negative feelings you have of yourself that have taken authority over your life. Seriously, how can you take good care of yourself when you have poor self-regard, shame, hate, doubt, and sorrow? It is also a great description of dislodging toxic relationships from your life.

So, what causes a person to not love themselves? There are many reasons, such as the person does not feel worthy of being loved. Maybe they grew up not feeling loved. Possibly, there was too much focus on their flaws, mistakes, and their insecurities. Those mistakes haunt them and leave them with regrets they do not know how to get release from. That person may think too much about what others think of them and may have limited or no experience with healthy relationships. They may be Gus Groany or feel like Ursula Unlucky. With all those constant complaints, how could one possibly love themselves? I want you to feel like Baxter Blessed and Freda Fortunate. Strive to be Gracey Growing and Leroy Learning.

If you are a trauma survivor, then that explains why you may be struggling a bit with self-care and self-love. I understand that people, things, situations, and events in your world have hurt you and you sometimes would prefer not having any attention, even being reclusive. Your sense of feeling safe has been taxed emotionally. Thus, you may have chosen to escape. Exposure to violence, living with unmanaged mental illness, either yours or those in the household, or living with addictions can cause trauma and its resulting effects on the psyche. There are other events, such as natural disasters, accidents, deaths, incarceration, financial losses, and even bullying. The result is to numb oneself and just come up with coping skills for survival, not self-care, much less self-love. If you feel dead inside, it will take some work to understand and

---

learnersdictionaries.com/us/definition/english/dislodge?q=dislodge.

regain your sense of self. There is the trust issue as well as who you can trust, as those who you thought were trustworthy in the past proved to be the opposite of that. This, unfortunately, makes the survivor not ask for support and adds to feelings of loneliness.

Maybe your leech is you have allowed the pain of your trauma or mental illness to be so emotionally extreme that you choose to take it out on yourself. I am talking about intentional self-harm. It is a coping mechanism but a very unhealthy one. I said choose because if you choose to self-injure, then you can choose not to self-injure. You have decided that to be the way to release feelings of pain, anxiety, shame, guilt, anger, grief, and self-hate. Stop the self-punishment! What has happened to you is not your fault. We all have flaws and faults. There is nothing helpful about focusing on them. When you hurt yourself, I get it that you release some tension, but the painful emotions return again, so how is that working? You will also see it increases your shame, guilt, and self-hate feelings. Depression is going to continue to be your negative best bud. Your self-esteem will take a hit big time. You keep that up over and over, and the leech will continue to stay with you. You are not growing through adversity, and you are not gaining personal strength and resiliency. I want you to love yourself and take care of yourself. Please get with a mental health specialist who specializes in getting to what is behind the self-injury.

Giving care to oneself shows you can be capable of giving it to others. You are responsible for yourself, so don't neglect yourself. When you show yourself loving care, you will develop confidence, which has its own rewards. Your social relationships will improve, and that really does add to the quality of one's life. Taking proper care of yourself gives you that feeling of control instead of the negative feelings that came with the out-of-control events that happened that you could do nothing about.

A big part of self-care is to get some solitude when needed. That means alone time, and everybody needs it. It means "refresh your soul" time. With it, perspective is gained, creativity increases, stress and depression decrease, and it helps you get to know yourself that you have worth and value.

Jesus showed us he took time to rest, eat, have fellowship with others, and pray. He needed communion time with His Father God. We are so much better at dealing with life's challenges when we cast the cares. And there are so many of them. We have the greatest listener and problem solver in the world caring for us. In His presence, a person can feel relief from life's hardships and that they can carry on knowing they are so greatly loved.

When Jesus was given the news that His relative John the Baptist had been beheaded, He withdrew by boat to a solitary place (Matthew 14:13). I believe He needed time to grieve. We have so many things that grieve us. We can minimize that sorrow by "going to a solitary place." That is very good self-charity.

SKILLS TO TRY:

1. Stop immediately comparing yourself to others. You will only create feelings of not being good enough. Why tear yourself up for what you don't have or that you don't look like something preferred? You are unique, and you have potential. Be about growing personally.

2. Concentrate on your good points and your strengths. Celebrate what is positive about yourself. Accept imperfections. Change only what you desire to change, and it is possible to do so.

3. Encourage yourself. What would a good friend do in

your circumstances?

4. Stop criticism of yourself and be warm and understanding when you fail or feel inadequate. Acknowledge where you have grown.

5. Are there any areas where your self-esteem has taken a hit? Can you improve in that area?

6. Let go of the past and visualize that baggage disappearing like luggage does on the airport carousel.

7. Self-charity includes positive self-talk. Catch yourself with negative self-talk and annihilate it. Replace it with positive self-talk, even if it seems foreign to do so.

8. Dislodge the leeches that have had power over you. The place where the sawing jaws have chewed emotionally on you, do wound care in the sense of loving, respecting, and valuing yourself and knowing you have worth. Have nothing less.

9. Are you doing those normal things like eating right, sleeping enough, and exercising? If you are abusing alcohol, drugs, or prescriptions or engaging in harmful behaviors, I recommend you see a counselor. Don't delay. You are worth getting to the bottom of the hurt and healing. Positive coping skills can be taught. Don't just read or hear them—apply them.

10. Do the things that feel good for you, such as bubble baths or showers, walking, being with people you can trust and are supportive, shopping responsibly, or spending time at the beach. Make a list and get it in your schedule.

11. Increase creativity. It will help you relax mentally. You

get to use both sides of your brain, the creative and logical side, which keeps you from ruminating about where life went wrong. That's why they have adult coloring books and classes such as painting and pottery, etc.... Music is good for the soul. Be careful what lyrics you listen to.

12. Start a list of two things you like about yourself in the morning, and then add two things in the evening. Repeat that the next day. By the end of the week, you will have twenty-eight things. Can you challenge yourself to do that for a month? It can be simple things like you like that you are tall, have blue eyes, have a sense of humor, are good with kids, that dogs and cats like you, or that you have a strong sense of style. I feel quite certain the leech will let go. How about going another month's worth?

"For you created my inmost being; you knit me together in my mother's womb. I praise you because I am fearfully and wonderfully made" (Psalm 139:13–14a, NIV).

Yes, you are fearfully and wonderfully made. We are a fabulous creation. God knows us and wants us to take good care of what He created.

RESPONSE:

AN EIGHT-LETTER WORD

It has only eight letters, but it will affect you considerably today. It also has everything to do with how your future plays out. That word is "attitude." Our attitude is a choice. It is an outward expression of an inward feeling or opinion. A negative attitude is a disposition or feeling that is not constructive, cooperative, or optimistic.

> *"When my attitude is right, there is no barrier too high, no valley too deep, no dream too extreme, no challenge too great for me."*
>
> **Charles W. Swindoll**

Attitude has a lot to do with stress. Attitude will draw people to us or away from us. Really, if you see on your phone that Albert Awful Attitude is calling, there is a strong possibility you will not want to answer it. If you are Pam Pessimistic, you probably do not have many or any friends and are not too fun to be around. A negative attitude can result in feeling helpless, hopeless, anxious, and depressed. That, in itself, can lead to chronic stress, which can upset one's hormones and deplete the brain chemistry needed for happiness. And with all seriousness, it can decrease how many years you live.

People with a negative outlook have thoughts where they expect the worst and create problems that do not exist. If your self-talk and attitude are negative, you perceive things as more stressful. If one perceives a situation as too difficult or unfair, then they are making it more stressful to deal with it, so perception plays a large role. People even beat themselves up emotionally when they fail to change their negative point of view. One can be hypervigilant and choose to isolate themselves.

I never want to be insensitive to the plight that trauma caused. It is rather common after trauma to have a negative outlook. It is common to look at the world through a lens of gloom. It is hard to see the sunshine and rainbows. One can be cynical. That means a person has a disbelief about other people's motivations, that others acted selfishly, and thus their own personal belief is skewed to being pessimistic and distrustful. After all, it is quite understandable since you likely were deceived and hurt and are now angry. One feels vulnerable, and a cynical attitude makes a person feel like they are protecting themselves. It also causes a "me against the world" attitude. If you feel like people respond to you with wrong motives, you don't end up asking for help, which, with the right people, would greatly improve your life. Being cynical also means you are choosing to keep your distance, so how is that developing meaningful relationships? Your negative view of the world could be a precursor to depression. Healing will be delayed.

Rachel Woods put out an informative article titled "Possible Reasons Behind Your Negative Attitude."[11] They are:

1. We don't want to be disappointed. We have been disappointed by people or situations in the past, and now we "protect" ourselves by expecting the worst.

---

11 Rachel Woods, *Possible Reasons Behind Your Negative Attitude.* LMHC for PsychCentral (November 2019).

2. We've had role models (possibly our parents) with negative attitudes. We've picked up their approach towards life and made it our habit as well, rather than working on deliberately developing our personal, proactive, and resilient perspective.

3. We don't want to be rejected. If we fear that other people might not approve of us, we decide (either consciously or unconsciously) to beat them to the punch and "not like them first."

4. If we can't do something perfectly, we are afraid to try it at all. If we can't please everyone, we don't see the point of being agreeable to anyone at all.

5. We set unrealistic expectations or try to change too much at one time. Then, when we encounter an obstacle, we overreact and possibly give up on our plan, which reinforces a negative attitude.

6. We think that any uncomfortable feeling is unwarranted and a sign of weakness on our part. This means we give up on ourselves. What's most important is the lens through which we view ourselves, other people, and the world, for the most part.

7. We think that fear or anger will energize and motivate us to change. Actually, although such emotions may kick-start an adrenalin rush and possible frenzied action in the short run, over the long term, they can run us down, impair our immune system, and contribute to depression and anxiety.

8. We are exceptionally sensitive to emotional or physical discomfort. Some of us are just more sensitive than others and have a lower pain threshold. This can contribute to negativity.

9. We have experienced significant trauma, hardships, or failures.

10. We're subconsciously replaying an issue with an authority figure or someone who controlled us—a syndrome known as "repetition compulsion." We are trying to work out a different ending.

11. We're used to being the victim rather than an agent of change. We feel that finger-pointing absolves us of the responsibility of taking action and changing what we can. We forgot that "that was then, and this is now," and we may have more tools at our disposal than we did earlier in our lives.

12. We want to be in control. In a way, determining ahead of time that things will not work out gives us a feeling of predictability.

13. We're *HALT*—which stands for "hungry," "angry," "lonely," or "tired." Any of these (and especially a combination of these factors) can fuel irritability, impatience, and despondency.

14. We suffer from clinical depression or chemical imbalance.

15. We have a medical condition that predisposes us to depression or anxiety.

I WILL ADD SOME OTHER THOUGHTS:

16. You feel negative about yourself and reinforce that with expressions like "Nobody would love me" or "I am too damaged." You struggle with a general sense of who you are and that you are undeserving of good things.

17. You believe the trauma is all your fault. This could play out in that you don't develop healthy relationships as you don't want to get blamed for anything.

18. You wrestle with guilt and shame on a regular basis.

19. You had an adverse childhood experience (ACE), and that has carried over into adulthood.

20. You have trust issues. It is understandable that people you thought you could trust ended up betraying you, manipulating you, controlling you, deceiving you, or injuring you emotionally or physically. There may have been things such as someone stealing your money or items, damaging your belongings, hurting your pet, or using the rent money for inappropriate activities, leaving you holding the bag of impossibilities. Even if given a compliment, you may not trust if it is sincere.

I have included those twenty points mentioned because if you are a trauma survivor, you may be predisposed to an attitude of emptiness and that life "sucks" because it has been very hard. I will not minimize how difficult and life-altering the events have been in your life. Trauma is different for everyone. One person may be overwhelmed with negative feelings, and another may be withdrawn and feel nothing but numbness. You may even just have a feeling like you are perpetually lost in a state of "I don't know what to do." You may feel chaotic in your head space sometimes. But I don't want you to stay in that state. You are not alone, and help in these pages will give you the insight to move from a negative outlook to one where you experience some optimism and hope for your happiness.

There was a Bible character named Nabal who seemed to be a negative character (1 Samuel 25). He is described as surly and mean. He got into an unreasonable, erroneous assumption about David possibly being a slave trying to break away from his master when David was only asking for some hospitality. Nabal was rich and stingy, but there was no need for his attitude, especially since David had protected Nabal's shepherds when they were in the wilderness. David felt insulted and angry and thus instructed four hundred men to get their swords for potential battle. Fortunately, Nabal's wife, Abigail, was informed of the precariously dangerous situation, and she came to save the day and, actually, many lives. I will call her Awesome Abigail (1 Samuel 25).

Let's look at Abigail's attitude. She seemed to have no fear. She was selfless as she acted quickly to save her people. She responded with great wisdom by providing rations of food for David's men. She was courageous and generous in spite of her challenges. When she arrived, she bowed respectfully. David said she had good judgment as his plan was to take revenge by killing all the males belonging to Nabal. The crisis was averted due to her smooth and brave actions.

Abigail informs David that Nabal is wicked and a fool, and folly goes with him. She returns home to find Nabal acting like a happy drunk. Abigail informed him the next day about the events that happened with David, and "his heart failed him, and he became like a stone." It adds the Lord struck him dead about ten days later. Oh my, God does what God does, and vengeance belongs to Him.

A negative attitude is a difficult habit to change. Is it quite possible that it has been years since you had any positive thoughts? A pessimistic attitude will weigh you down like a brick on your shoulder. People with a bad attitude look at what is negative in other people and situations. They see limitations. They also believe there is nothing to look forward to in the future. Therefore, they have trouble making long-term goals. Changing from negative to positive will bring you some needed cheer from scenarios that have been very tough. It will also help you fight depression and anxiety that could be prevalent. For those who have been injured or ill, it will help you strengthen your immunity and heal quicker. Energy will improve. Having a positive attitude will help you see the world in a better light. We can all use that, and people may thus see us in a better light.

It does not mean there will be less stress, so you can think in a more hopeful way, but it may help you look for strategies to improve the situation. You might even move out of denial and into how you can recover from the trauma. Wouldn't it seem good to look at life from the perspective of the glass is half full, not half empty? Possibilities do exist. Nabal, in the story above, jumped to conclusions where it could have been disastrous, and a massacre would have ensued.

SKILLS TO TRY:

1. First, be willing to change. Take responsibility for what you say and what you do.

2. Don't complain, blame others, hold grudges, and don't look for the shortcomings in others.

3. Avoid negative people. That group probably fuels one's negative attitude. Surround yourself with positive people. It is a good idea to ask someone to help you be accountable when you slip up. Other trusted people's perspective is usually enlightening.

4. Look at your strengths and accomplishments. Don't dwell on the negative events, even though they may loom right in front of you. Abigail, in the story above, seemed to be married to a hot-headed, unreasonable

man. Her strengths and wisdom saved the day. Develop you.

5. Keep self-care going. Start your day off right by telling yourself something positive. End the day with something positive. Anticipation or having something to look forward to is a positive emotion that helps the doldrums.

6. Have hope. It will help you see the best in the worst. You may need to dig deep.

7. Invite laughter into your life like an enjoyable best friend. It increases the feel-good hormones. It helps relieve pain. If you crack jokes and tell funny stories, it helps fight the stress and its negative hormone cortisol. It relieves tension and thus helps you relax. There are short-term and long-term benefits as well. After trauma, laughter will help a person feel less like a victim and more like life can be good again. It will help people live in the moment and be less burdened with all the heaviness. It helps rebalance the brain from the gloom and doom to peace and more carefree hope.

8. To combat cynicism, feel what you are feeling, whether frustration, anger, or pain. It is also hard to feel your feelings when they were quelled as a child, so you have to learn how to do that. Create compassion for self and for others. Try to understand that when one feels like the world is not a good place or other people have wrong motivations, a lot of times, they are coming from a place of hurt as well. Down deep inside, you do know the world is a beautiful place, and it is not out to get you and ruin your life. Create safety and security for yourself and look for the beauty. Do not rob your-

self of joy.

9. Look at the twenty points above one by one and ask yourself where you need to tweak things. Take your time with this. Incorporate family, friends, and a counselor if needed.

"Do not conform to the pattern of this world, but be transformed by the renewing of your mind" (Romans 12:2, NIV).

The apostle Paul is saying not to pattern your life like those around you. The believer must live in the secular world but not be caught up in it. The Holy Spirit works from within by renewing our minds. One's old worldly thinking needs to change to godly thinking. Exposing our thinking by taking in the word of God is a significant part of that process. Do you have the indwelling Spirit to help?

RESPONSE:

EYELIDS, HUMPS, AND SPIT

No book on trauma should be complete without addressing resilience. It's that important. It means the ability to adapt to change, bounce back from difficulty, or, in general, recover from setbacks or tragedy. I want that for you.

The title refers to a camel. The dromedary camel has one hump, and the Bactrian camel has two humps. The humps are for storage. They contain body fat—almost eight pounds of it. Camels are built for survival. They can go long distances without resources as well as survive extreme cold or hot. They also have a third eyelid, which protects their eyes from blowing sand, and they have two rows of long lashes. They can even shut their nostrils during sandstorms. Those thick lips are for helping them eat things most other animals wouldn't, such as plants with thorns. Spitting is their defensive tactic when they feel threatened. That spit also contains contents from the stomach. Camels also make deep, throaty bellows, and they moan and groan. When their backs are loaded, and they have to get up off the ground, they groan to get to their feet. Camels can experience trauma when treated badly or when they have been injured by humans, wild animals, or vehicles.

Let's compare and learn from Carl Camel or Camille Camel. If you are the human Carl or Camille, then what did you pick out from this information? I will help you think it through. What do you think would help with your resiliency? What do you think needs to be stored in those humps? When the sandstorms of life come, and you have gone without resources for a significant amount of time, then you need to cope, be hardy, and be able to rebound. Sandstorms actually hurt. You have hurt as well. Store coping skills for the hard walk through it. Maybe you should store practical things such as food and water. You could also store the word of God, as that would be highly encouraging.

How do you go the distance like the camel? Practicing self-compassion is a good one. That means you will comfort yourself emotionally, physically, mentally and take care of your social and spiritual needs. You will encourage yourself. You will be kind to yourself. After all, you live with yourself one hundred and sixty-eight hours a week. Be very kind to yourself. I can't say it enough. There are some stressors that just can't be eliminated, so if you take care of yourself, you can manage them much easier. Some of those long-suffering circumstances require endurance and patience as we either live with others who are testy or they just need us and pull on us to take care of them.

You may short-change your ability to go the distance if you carry around self-pity. For a while, you can cry, be glum, and have some anger, but unfortunately, feeling sorry for oneself seems to take on a life of its own, and when that happens, it takes over. Keep that going, and you have self-pity majorly in charge instead of you. It's your life; you must be in charge, not the "poor little ole me" thinking. It will make you stay angry, feel needy, deprived, down on your luck, and at a disadvantage. That "woe is me" thinking is a statement of despair from a person who is very sad and has no hope. That is never true. We always have hope. Start with a hug to yourself. Be with healthy friends to build your sense of belonging. Camels are very social and like to stay in groups.

As mentioned, camels have an extra eyelid. Be observant. This does not mean to be hypervigilant. That will just cause you anxiety and worry. See a better perspective and realize that camels are tall, so those eyes have an advantage point. Keep your sights on your future and that it will get better. See higher and see what God sees. That is your advantage point. He sees you overcoming the pressure, abuse, heat, cold, and environmental harshness. Don't go where you will be triggered, and don't be with people who are negative. Get away from Brutus Brutal and Monica Mocking. Tia Tirade can't be fun to be with. That would get old.

Camels can shut their nostrils, which in itself is an amazing way that God made the animal. Sand can actually stick to your skin pretty well. And those big lips, well, maybe movie stars think they are pretty on humans, but...no comment. About resiliency, those lips let the camel graze on about anything without getting hurt, and those lips help them conserve moisture. Let your lips speak positive statements. Affirmations such as "Come on, you can do this" or "Body, get up, go to work." Make a list, and when you tell yourself these positive remarks, it will go from the head to the heart to some motivation.

Spit, really? Cope, don't spit! Be smart. Use common sense. Don't be Spike Spit, be Corine Cope. Camels are resourceful. They can take the heat. Resilient people can go the distance. They can even serve people. We can serve the Lord, who will heal us from trauma and even make it not hurt so we can move forward and help others. Paying forward feels good. God does not waste the events that happen to us. Case in point: my negative events have turned into two books about helping others. Resilient people have learned to take the heat (cope with a stressful situation, intense pressure, or endure).

The dromedary camels have thick pads of skin on their chest

and knees so they can sit on very hot sand. To walk, the camel moves both legs on the same side at the same time. My fun memory is the potato sack race, where your leg and a partner's leg are in the sack or pillow case, and you must move together to get to the finish line. Aah, find someone who will move together with you and go the distance. You know, the thick and thin friends and family. Camels are capable of going short bursts of forty miles for an hour. The camel does not even sweat until about 106 degrees Fahrenheit. We have all been in very "hot" places where we just needed an escape physically and emotionally. This gives a person time to cope with the hardship or take the time to deal with the reality of one's "heated situation." It will reduce the stress we feel from the circumstances and the burnout from going through the short and long bursts and help us regain our strength. This is self-care, and you need it and deserve it.

There was a time I wanted to escape just for a short while, but I was so very responsible in taking care of my kids that I would not. I felt like it, though. So, be responsible. Look at what would happen if you escaped. Maybe you can escape to pray, get energized, or get practical help. As a comparison, thick-skinned people (those who are not easily upset, are tough, and can roll with the punches) deal with abuse better than those who are sensitive or let things get to them easily. The thin-skinned person will respond to physical and emotional pain more easily than those who express a thicker skin. Thick-skinned people are mentally tough. The caveat is to not accept abuse. Spiritually speaking, we have been made with the capacity to withstand against the enemy of our soul, the devil, by putting on the armor of God (Ephesians 6).

SKILLS TO TRY:

1. To help you to be suited for life, including harsh environments, you will need stamina, adaptability, perse-

verance, resiliency, and strength.

A. Stamina is the ability to sustain prolonged physical or mental effort. You want your body to improve oxygen supply. Being consistent in exercising will help develop this. Foods that help are fruits, whole-wheat bread, brown rice, oats, and nuts. Apple juice is good to drink. Nix the alcohol. After exercise, have a banana. Vitamin B is good for building stamina.

B. Adaptability is the ability to change your ideas or behavior in order to deal with new situations. You will need to be flexible. Be positive and exhibit positive self-talk. That positivity will go far to help you not feel like you can't make it. It's a great habit that will take you through everything in life easier. Think ahead and keep in mind safety. Give up any attitude of being disgruntled even though it has been tough. It just won't help to stay that way. Adaptability will prepare you for the coming challenges. I know you have had enough of what is unfair, but like life, there will be more. This next time, though, you are armed with skills. You will need to be open to having a lot of resources to help you in the harsh days of life. Have strategies in place for the rough patch days, and you have to face uncertainty.

C. Perseverance is persistence in doing something despite the difficulty, delay, failure, or opposition. That is also being steadfast. It's your grit and determination. It will help you stay motivated when things get too hard and you want to quit and take an easier route. Don't think of throwing in the towel when you are almost through your semester, you are close to getting a raise, or you have almost set up the money to leave for a safer situation. Dopamine in your brain will need to be increased so you can receive the rewards of making it through the setbacks. It will include engaging in activities that make you feel happy or calm. Eat foods high in magnesium and tyrosine-rich foods. Try protein-rich foods such as turkey, eggs, dairy, and legumes. Try listening to music, meditation/ prayer, and being in the sunlight.

D. Resiliency—as mentioned at the beginning of this section. The things that help develop it are to have a good support system and strong connections with people who are positive and loving. Spend time with Linda Light-hearted and Pepper Peppiness. Milo Misery will keep you down. Developing a self-image that is good and a positive attitude will take you through the desert places. Have self-confidence so you believe in yourself to go further than you think you can. Change will be something we must deal with forever, and along with that comes stress. Planning ahead, if possible, will help buffer the changes.

E. Strength. Camels are very strong. They can carry up to nine hundred pounds. Strength, according to the Oxford Dictionary, is the quality or state of being physically strong and the capacity of an object or substance to withstand great force or pressure.[12] That translates as being tough; a good

---

12 "Strength." strength, noun—Definition, pictures, pronunciation and usage notes | Oxford Advanced Learner's Dictionary at OxfordLearnersDic-

kind of tough, a solid person, sturdy and durable. Yes, we want that. We need to be able to stand against pressure. Focus on where you managed pressure successfully in the past. Don't bite your fingernails off. Instead, deep breathe. You need the oxygenated air. Under pressure, your prefrontal cortex doesn't function at its best.

Strength is not all physical. We need emotional strength to manage emotions. It is difficult to be around people who don't manage their emotions. Those people are argumentative, have outbursts, they make it hard to have a positive relationship with them, and they seem to not be very aware of other people's feelings. They can lose their temper easily and have low frustration tolerance. They also don't take criticism well; they take things personally. They are people like Enzo Energy Zappin'. Some people take our emotional strength and leave us feeling exhausted and even depressed. Sometimes, around these people, I feel like I walk on hot coals, and they are like a vampire eating away at my kindness. This happens because we let other people drain us, and we are too drained to deal with them. Maybe if you allow this, you are a people pleaser. The solution is not to try and change other people but to focus on building yourself into a strong tower and setting boundaries.

There is also mental strength. Take in this paragraph by Amy Morin:[13]

tionaries.com. Accessed September 3, 2023. https://www.oxfordlearnersdictionaries.com/definition/english/strength?q=strength.
13 Amy Morin. "13 Things Mentally Strong People Don't Do: Take Back Your Power, Embrace

That involves being aware of your emotions, learning from your painful experiences, and living according to your values. It includes regulating your thoughts so you train your brain to think in a helpful way. This means you will need to ignore self-doubt or replace self-criticism with self-compassion. One will need to manage their emotions. This means that being aware of your emotions allows you to understand how those feelings influence the way you think and behave. It can involve embracing emotions—even when they are uncomfortable—or it may be about acting contrary to your emotions, when those feelings don't serve you well. Behaving productively means choosing to take action that will improve your life, even when you struggle with motivation or delayed gratification, which is key to becoming mentally strong.

1. There were five main areas to examine in the above. Take each one and examine where you may need to tweak your life and build stamina, adaptability, perseverance, resiliency, and physical, emotional, and mental strength.

"Do not store up for yourself treasures on earth, where moth and rust destroy, and where thieves break in and steal. But store up for yourself treasures in heaven, where moth and rust do not destroy, and where thieves do not break in and steal" (Matthew 6:19–20, NIV).

The camel needs to store fat, but we need to store up treasures in heaven. There is no bank in heaven. We are to store up what is valuable to God. What is valuable to God? I would say, people. We are to love people, and that may include using what we have to help them. We need to be what we are supposed to be, do what we are called to do, and do it with the right heart as well. We must never forget our greatest treasure is a personal relationship with Jesus.

Change, Face Your Fears, and Train Your Brain for Happiness and Success." HarperCollins, 2014.

RESPONSE:

_____

_____

_____

_____

_____

_____

_____

_____

_____

_____

_____

_____

_____

_____

_____

_____

_____

_____

_____

_____

_____

_____

KEEP SWIMMING
AND RESILIENCY

I must write a bit more about resiliency because it is so badly needed for anyone who has been through trauma. Actually, everyone just needs this skill. People will their whole life need to know how to recover or rebound from challenges. Recuperate, overcome, rally and comeback are also good words. Whatever word you like, it will involve believing in yourself and adapting to difficult circumstances. If you were exposed to trauma or trying to prevent any further exposure, resiliency skills are a valuable tool. Even if you have good coping skills, trauma can be so overwhelming that it takes over. Learning some skills will help you be less susceptible to anxiety and depression.

Let's look at resiliency from the fictional characters from the 2003 movie *Finding Nemo*.[14] Nemo is a little clownfish whose mother and all his sibling fish (still eggs) were eaten by a barracuda. So, he grew up with an overprotective dad clownfish named Marlin. As a parent, it is understandable after major life events to be overprotective, angry, depressed, fearful, worried, anxious, etc. Against his father's warning, Nemo ventured into an area of the ocean where he was "kidnapped" by a scuba diver. Much time passed, which included scary and negative events, and Nemo end-

14 Stanton, Andrew, and Lee Unkrich. Finding Nemo. 2003. Emeryville, CA: Pixar Animation Studios.

ed up in a fish tank in a dentist's office with a misfit group of other captured fish who all longed to go back to the ocean. This little fish is so likable, smart, and has a determination that is really resiliency. On the negative side, it seems like he does not like being told what to do. His father frustrates him. He has been through several major losses—the attack on his mother and siblings. He has a disability: a deformed fin.

Nemo's father, Marlin, is fearful, anxious, rather wound tightly, unhappy, and negative. This dad fish is domineering but is very tenacious and loves his son so much that he went through an extreme amount of challenges that could have killed him to try and get to his son even when he did not know where he was. To find his son, Marlin's love overtook his fears. Love didn't stop. Sounds like the Lord, who didn't stop reaching out to us either. Marlin ends up learning courage, persistence, resiliency, and the lesson of letting go.

Marlin picks up a new friend fish along the way, a blue tang surgeonfish named Dory. Dory is sympathetic to Marlin's cause to find his son and offers to be a resource. She readily admits to him she has a bad case of short-term memory loss. Marlin finds her frustrating and annoying sometimes, but she is a happy-go-lucky kind of fish in spite of her disability.

I will put this all together for you so you will be able to relate. Marlin has been through it as he witnessed a vicious attack and loss of his wife, fish, and all the eggs about to hatch. It could have been a couple hundred eggs. He was knocked unconscious. After that, he is a mess of anxiety, worry, and fear. His love propels him to find his son, and that drama involves looking into unknown treacherous waters. He encounters a threatening shark that invited him and his companion, Dory, to what seemed like a "fishy" twelve-step meeting. Everything was okay until the shark smelled blood, and they ended up swimming furiously for their lives. Not only does he fight off the sharks, but he also has to save himself and his new friend from an angry angler fish. He also escapes from an explosion and ends up having to get free from a bunch of jelly-fish. The terrifying ordeals continued as the two were swallowed by a whale. Fortunately, the whale discharges the pair from its blowhole. Marlin and Dory are so close to finding Nemo when they are attacked by seagulls as well, as a pelican grabs them. Marlin fights to not be eaten and ends up on a dock, grasping for his last breath. A different pelican, this one helpful shows Marlin and Dory where Nemo has been held captive and on display in a tank in a dental office. Nemo is belly up and looks dead. But is he dead?

The angler fish is very creepy-looking and has lots of menacing teeth. It has what looks like a bioluminescent fishing pole protruding from its head to catch its food. That "pole" is full of bacteria. Angler fish can be a reminder to navigate through the darkness and keep allowing the "light" to shine and guide. Watch out for those who bring "bacteria" into our lives. Do you have a parasitic relationship with anyone?

Sharks remind a person to keep moving. They do not stop, so they symbolize tenacity to keep going. Sharks are definitely fearless. They are very focused and powerful. To go through what Marlin did, he needed this. Let's be creative and say that an explosion like the one Marlin and Dory went through represents an individual who has bottled up their emotions and doesn't cope with the tough parts of life events, so "explodes" with emotions. That is not positive as it would cause something that sounds more like excessive anger, and thus, some regrettable response would likely follow it. There is a proper way to handle the difficult side of life, and that is to express your feelings "without blowing your top." Of course, that is easier said than done, especially when issues have not been resolved, they go on for a lengthy time, and one is overwhelmed. In this fishy tale, the emotions are loss/grief, trauma, sadness, anxiety, fear, and the unknown. God gave us emotions, but we need to learn to control them—to respond, not react.

I have negative memories of jellyfish. In the summers while growing up, I would swim in the Northumberland Strait, which is a body of water between Nova Scotia and Prince Edward Island, Canada. I have had a few encounters where I did not see the jellyfish and was stung. They leave a burning pain. They are toxic, so I will liken them to having toxic relationships. I can't say enough that if you have been traumatized, you need to avoid toxic relationships. The problem is many don't recognize they are in a relationship with someone who emotionally manipulates them. Possibly, this is due to childhood, where their role models were controllers. Some can't get away from toxic people as they are financially dependent on them. Do you see the signs in yourself that maybe you are with a toxic person? That would be you having trust issues, self-esteem issues, feeling insecure, paranoid, helpless, anxious, depressed, and maybe numb and confused.

Marlin and Dory were attacked by seagulls. Seagulls are beautiful birds, but they are scavengers and prey on fish, insects, mice, birds, and mollusks. They like to hang around pelicans to steal their food. They are quite intelligent. They will attack humans and animals and inflict injuries. So, what do you expect the comparison to be? Those who have experienced trauma may feel like mollusks, clams, scallops, or oysters that have been injured by seagulls. How? They dig in the sand or surf to create this heist of what they grabbed, then fly up to a height they cleverly figured out worked and drop their catch like a hot potato onto a hard surface to break it open. So, watch out for scavengers, those who exploit others as they are selfish and users. They are people who take advantage of you when you are vulnerable. They take, but they don't give in a relationship. In trying to heal from trauma, people may begin to try and open up to others again, and there is the chance of being vulnerable and taken advantage of. Listen to your instincts—if you smell something rotten in a relationship, then it probably is rotten. It is difficult to sometimes trust your instincts when you have been hurt.

SKILLS TO TRY:

1. Stay determined. Nemo jammed up the tank filter as he had a plan to escape his current restricted life. He was not letting anything get in his way. Sounds like purpose. Determining to finish what needs to get done will keep you focused and not feeling so lost and sad in life.

2. Nemo had a disability that did not seem to deter him from doing whatever he wanted to do. He even called his deformed fin a "lucky fin." Can you look at any mental or physical disabilities with respect and dignity? Dory seemed to be quite forthright with her short-term memory disability and did not let it define her. She seemed to be strong and friendly. If you have a disability, it does not have to be disabling. Always play to your strengths and educate others. The fish from the fish tank told Nemo, "Your differences don't define you." Let God be your ability in your disability. Love yourself.

3. Dory told Merlin to relax and take a deep breath. I know you know this, but it is easy to forget when caught up in drama. Taking deep breaths will increase the oxygen to your brain, which stimulates the parasympathetic nervous system and helps you get to a calmer state.

4. Merlin and Dory were swallowed by a whale and were

so resilient and determined that while in the whale's stomach, they kept hitting the whale to get out. Don't quit. They were blown out of the blowhole. Dory reminded Merlin to keep his eye on his goal.

5.   Nemo also was in a bag of water. He was so bent on escaping from his dire situation that he pushed against the bag. At least do something. Keep pushing. Staying stagnant will cause you to stop moving forward and make you feel like you are not up to it. Give yourself the "one, two, you can do it" speech.

6.   Dory said, "I don't want to forget." The thing about trauma is in healing. You may need to talk about those traumatic memories so you can move forward. Sometimes, remembering them will help you not be in that situation again, so it is a protective measure. I recommend that if this is a challenging area for you, a mental health therapist would be beneficial.

7.   Think of a (fish) tank as your environment. List the things that need to change so you can be happy and feel safe. Prioritize that list and start with the first one. Get support—have a dependable circle of friends and family. Merlin and Dory had turtle friends that helped. If you didn't grow up in an environment that validated you, it may have left you feeling like life is out of control, and you stay stressed. The little turtle, Squirt, acted like his dad, fearless and easy-going. His dad, Crush, helped Merlin move past his fears. He was carefree and had fun. Merlin needed to learn that. Crush told them to hang on as the current was about to get rough. Squirt also tells them to hang on and be careful. Isn't that good advice from a senior and a junior? Hang

on with the rough currents of life. Remember, persevere in spite of any odds, and be wary.

8. About those clever seagulls, or we can say manipulative scammers who prey on the vulnerable. The seagulls have great eyesight, so keep your vision of your goals and be on the lookout, not in a paranoid way but in a smart way, and avoid people who treat you wrong. Keep working on yourself, what you want to be, and where you want to go in life. Give no regard to other people's negative opinions about you. Explain to supportive people what your needs are, and I expect you will get a lot of support in return. Give yourself some compassion. Don't give your power away, especially to thoughtless people or those who want to be like seagulls who try and be superior and will break you.

9. Keep swimming. When Dory was caught in a net, Merlin and Nemo told all the fish to swim down. To swim down meant at that time to swim downward to go against the pull so they could weigh it downward and break the net, which they did. For us, it means to stay moving in the struggles we face, stay afloat, fight the current, move through it, or like life you are going down. Consider it also means to resist or prevail over what comes against you. By the way, prevail means to prove you are stronger than opposing forces. Yes, you can overcome. Dory had a great quote: "When life gets you down, you know what you gotta do? Just keep swimming." Tell yourself what Dory encouraged Merlin to do, which was to keep trying and not give up.

10. Be part of a strong community where there is good

teamwork. It will build resilience. It will encourage personal growth and reduce stress. It will cause one to feel empowered, and self-confidence is gained. It causes people to learn from each other and get things done, as well as overcome obstacles. Merlin and Dory would not have gotten to Nemo without teamwork. Dory would not have gotten out of the net without the encouragement. Name someone who you consider a good support system. Does that relationship need further development, or is it good? Can you add another person to your support network?

11. To respond and not react: Take time to collect yourself. Move that energy where you feel like exploding into something that is physical and safe to do. Listen to yourself so you don't jump to conclusions. Don't allow your emotions to control you. You need to be in control. If you can build resilience, you will combat the stress and pressure from the crisis. Tap into your strengths, which will help you respond, not react. Believe in yourself and tell yourself you are coping to the best of your ability, but be ever working on developing healthy coping skills so you can adapt and return to something that feels normal. Even though you might not want to hear this, when life is down the drain, be optimistic if you can. That way, you will see your negative situation as temporary rather than leaving you with no hope. Staying motivated will build resilience so you can cope with emotional turbulence.

"Though the fig tree does not bud and there are no grapes on the vine, though the olive crop fails and the fields produce no food, though there are no sheep in the pen and no cattle in the stalls, yet

I will rejoice in the Lord, I will be joyful in God my Savior" (Habakkuk 3:17–18, NIV).

Habakkuk was expressing a lot of nothingness but was able to rejoice in the Lord in spite of it all. Things may fail and not go well, but keep your faith and have joy in the Lord for the things He has done. Trust God to keep His promises. He is far better than all that looks lost and all the suffering. He is also very aware of us and what is happening. He will work it out for our good and for His glory.

RESPONSE:

_____

_____

_____

_____

_____

_____

_____

_____

_____

_____

_____

_____

_____

_____

_____

_____

_____

_____

_____

_____

_____

_____

PERSEVERANCE IN SPITE OF ADVERSITY

I cannot help but use the soldiers who serve as sentinels at the Tomb of the Unknown Soldier as an example of determination and honor. This monument at Arlington National Cemetery is dedicated to the four service members who have not been identified. They are known only by God. Each one of the soldiers represents World War I, World War II, Korea, and Vietnam. However, there are three now as the soldier that represented Vietnam had been identified, and a crypt cover was placed over it saying "Honoring and Keeping Faith with America's Missing Servicemen, 1958–1975." The practice of guarding the tomb started during the day in 1926 to keep people from climbing the tomb, and since 1937, it has been guarded twenty-four-seven.

The story that needs to be told is the perseverance of the sentinels who perform with the highest dedication twenty-four hours a day, seven days a week, and 365 days a year under any weather condition. They walk their sixty-three-foot path with no allowance for distractions and with no fear. When hurricanes Isabel, Irene, and Sandy were coming through, the sentinels were given a choice to suspend their duty, but they stood resolute in their "no way, sir." It was recorded that they were never put at risk in spite of their determination to fulfill their duty.

The sentinels have to undergo intensive training. The training lasts about seven to eight months. It is so rigorous that there is a ninety percent failure rate. According to Wikipedia,[15] 688 soldiers, since the late 1950s, have received the honored badge to distinguish their service.

The sentinel's creed is "My dedication to this sacred duty is total and wholehearted. In the responsibility bestowed on me never will I falter. And with dignity and perseverance my standard will remain perfection. Through the years of diligence and praise and the discomfort of the elements. I will walk my tour in humble reverence to the best of my ability. It is he who commands the respect I protect. His bravery that made us so proud. Surrounded by well-meaning crowds by day alone in the thoughtful peace of night, this soldier will, in honored glory, rest under my eternal vigilance."

Besides it being a very honored, selfless lifestyle to guard the Tomb of the Unknown Soldier, I want to correlate this to what perseverance is. Of course, I give my highest regard to the perfection and dedication of the sentinels and will use their stories with admiration and as an example of inspiration to others. This kind of perseverance gives a person purpose. It creates resilience when mental illness, physical disability, and history of trauma are one's cross to bear.

Research indicates that those who persevere towards their goals and don't quit have less depression and anxiety and can hold up under detrimental conditions. They have a sense of being in control in spite of their diagnosis' or what could be considered a cruel, unfair past. One must continue to believe that one's life has meaning. They can have an optimistic attitude and keep persevering in hopes that their setbacks will withstand the "elements" (the

---

15 *"Tomb of the Unknown Soldier (Arlington)."* Wikipedia, September 7, 2023. https://en.wikipedia.org/wiki/Tomb_of_the_Unknown_Soldier_(Arlington).

storms of life) like the sentinels.

Perseverance means you keep going in spite of obstacles. This would take willpower, which is the ability to control or restrain yourself, and the ability to resist instant gratification in order to achieve long-term goals.[16]

Life has the potential to drain about everything out of you. It is especially true if it just occurs ruthlessly over and over again. Focus on going forward and focus on self-improvement. Paul McCartney of the Beatles fame wrote a song called "Let It Be." Paul had a mother who died when he was fourteen years old. One night, when he was particularly troubled, he felt like his mother, named Mary, came to him in a dream and spoke words of wisdom (Songfacts). His song was aptly named "Let It Be." For us, that can translate to wise advice that we have to "let go" of our history and its negative grip. I realize that trauma is something you carry, and nobody should be so insensitive to tell you or expect you to "get over it," but you can learn to live with it, recover, and even thrive. I very much want that for you.

SKILLS TO TRY:

1. Try and get on your footpath. Walk it with perseverance and determination. You may not make it all the way down the path like the sentinels, but at least get on the mat. Even if you are in a wheelchair or using a walker or with injuries, seen or unseen due to abuse or accidents, make an attempt to get on the mat toward your life's path. There is no condemnation. A path can even be staying put and praying—your prayer path for yourself and others.

2. The second, third, and fourth paragraphs have key-

---

16 verywellmind.com, April 21, 2021.

words or phrases that I trust you picked out to try applying. I will help you pick them out. Have no distractions, no fear, be resilient, rigorously train, be dedicated, have dignity, diligence, perseverance, and don't falter. Some discomfort is involved. Do what you can to the best of your ability. Let's clarify: Change is hard and uncomfortable; after all, we get hurt, and wounds take time to heal, and then there are all those other things like lack of finances, paying rent, and the children's needs. Fear, check, it's there, understandable, it's about moving in the direction of self-confidence and calmness. It takes time, one step at a time. It also takes an element of trust. Take it easy on yourself emotionally. Training is learning, and somebody who is trustworthy and wise can do this to help a person get going. Dignity is your sense of pride and self-respect. Hold your head up. You are not broken; you are wounded. Your response section is for you to record how you can do these things.

3. Continue your search to find your purpose. For some, it might be taking care of family or serving the Lord. Maybe it is in helping others or volunteer work. What do you want to do when you get up in the day, or what do you feel passionate about? That is a clue. My first book, *Stuff Your Fanny Pack with Coping Skills*, has pages 287–306 on finding your purpose. This is extra important to find your purpose as trauma in a survivor's brain is in "protect mode." You may have been focused on surviving instead of achieving your goals and fulfilling your dreams, so do some self-discovery. Once you can move past the single desire to stay safe, then you will find it easier to move out with some risk-taking and achieve what you set up as your best-case scenario.

4. Believe in yourself. Make a benchmark, achieve it, and then go to the next level. For example, if you want your bachelor's degree, you need to get your two-year degree first. If you want better savings, start with something and add to it as regularly as you can. It does not matter if you are going at it slowly; you are going at it—so kudos to you; self-congratulations are in order.

5. Look at that definition of perseverance again—you keep going in spite of obstacles. Trauma affects motivation. It may have caused you to have learned helplessness. It makes a person not even bother to try. You are worth all the effort you can muster up. Loss of control, strength, courage, and hope have been lost. You watched it sail down the waterfall under tons of water. The task is this: what you think affects how you feel and how you feel you act out, so examine what you are thinking and if it is self-defeating and curtailing your success. Is there any area you need to tweak and make adjustments as you walk along your path? If it feels like you failed in any area, remember to adjust for the challenge and don't quit. Don't be afraid to fail. Don't let sadness, shame, or guilt take over. There is a learning curve. Small steps are still steps.

6. Don't isolate. Let the right people in to help and give you love and support. I understand that the horrible events you encountered, especially during childhood, may have caused some shame, and you expect rejection. However, don't compound that with isolation because it can often lead to depression, anxiety, increased substance abuse, and a host of medical conditions. Sometimes, people get pushed away under the false notion they need distance. I must call this self-sabotage.

Plan to talk to people you trust every day and share your feelings. There are hobbies to engage in and other activities you enjoy, so participate in them. I can advocate for rescuing a dog or cat, but if you do, be a great pet parent. You likely won't isolate as the animal needs a walk or playtime at a dog park.

"Write down the revelation and make it plain on tablets, though it lingers, wait for it; it will certainly come and will not delay" (Habakkuk 2:2a; 2:3b, NIV).

Write down where you want to go—your goals. Writing it down will make it more than just a thought, and it will keep it before you when things get hard, you want to quit, you get pulled in different directions, or you have a tough emotional day. Just like the sentinels who would never think of abandoning their responsibility or even their dreams, do the same.

RESPONSE:

_____

_____

_____

_____

_____

_____

_____

_____

_____

_____

_____

_____

_____

_____

_____

_____

_____

_____

_____

_____

_____

_____

_____

MS. J'S TRAUMAS

"There is a part of me that will always be broken." That was the last thing my interviewee said. It has resonated with me that it is profoundly true for those who have experienced trauma. But what about those who have gone through multiple traumas? Those who experience multiple traumatic events are likely to have high levels of post-traumatic stress disorder (PTSD), anxiety, and depression. Other symptoms are having a skewed sense of self-esteem, long-term difficulties in relationships, guilt, shame, trouble regulating emotions, and some hopelessness. After hearing Ms. J's story, I may even call it complex post-traumatic stress disorder. Here is Ms. J's remarkable story in her own words:

I went through domestic violence with my first husband. We were married for seven years, and all seven of those years, there was emotional abuse. We got along fine when dating, but after we married, his personality changed—he became distant and condescending. He gave me the cold shoulder but was sure to give me the put-downs. A friend saw red flags as my husband was nine years older and a recovering alcoholic. But I thought he was a new person. He started drinking again, and then the physical abuse started. Things deteriorated. He locked me out of the house when it was cold, and my two-year-old and four-year-old saw that. Another occasion was when he beat me with a plastic baseball bat while I was holding my two-year-old. He came at the both of us with a chair. It was a close call. I went to the doctor as my head was hurting, and I was diagnosed with a concussion from the bat to my head. He knew how to beat me and not leave marks.

On another occasion, I had made black beans, and he threw them at me. I hid at a neighbor's house with my kids. I got a restraining order. The neighbor witnessed him pick up a brick to shatter my car window, but he put it down. Again, he had been drinking. I got him out of the house, and now that he was gone, I was okay.

I joined the Air Force. My divorce was finalized a year or so after that. My first husband remarried, and he and his wife had the kids for the Thanksgiving weekend. They kept my kids, now aged eight and ten. I never got them back. I battled for years and years in court to get them back. They paid a lot of money to attorneys. He intentionally was trying to make me insane. I got visitation. He abused my son physically and mentally, but not my daughter. He beat me with a sledgehammer on my leg, and I was withering in pain. He only stopped as the dog jumped on me, and he did not want to hurt the dog. Part of me felt dead. I would wake up, and my mind played a video of that trauma. There was so much mental trauma. I sobbed a lot. How I coped was to catch myself when I was starting to spiral; I recognized that I was replaying the abuse. I relived that for years. Nowadays, I take medication, and I am determined to put one foot in front of the other.

The kidnapping of my children was my greatest trauma, and it went on for years. I also went through Hurricane Andrew in 1992, which caused significant damage. I was diagnosed with thyroid cancer at age thirty, and it is suspected that the thyroidectomy may have contributed to my losing my eyesight. I am diagnosed with Stargardt's disease (a form of macular degeneration), so I am considered legally blind. I can no longer drive, which brings on a host of challenges in and of itself.

My oldest son died in 2020 from a fentanyl overdose. He was thirty-five years old. I was devastated. I relived my abuse as he had been with the man who abused both of us. At that time, I leaned on people who were there to help me.

My other coping skills are when I relive the traumas, I catch myself and stop it. I tell myself it is ancient history. I practice awareness, which teaches you to identify what you are doing. I use an app that teaches guided meditation. I stay busy, and I find new things to do.

I function at sixty percent instead of one hundred percent. I want trauma survivors to live their lives and stay busy to help cope. The survivors should be patient with themselves and take baby steps. I regret putting myself in unsafe situations. I let my abuser get the best of me. For him, it was all about winning. I allowed my children to be my world, and in my custody dispute, life was not fair, and I got an injustice, so it is best to separate yourself a little as you could be easily manipulated. Looking back, I would have preserved my mental health better. The result of all of this is I went to law school and became an attorney to help other people with custody situations.

Just my two cents: bravo to Ms. J. That is paying forward. That is also great insight and employing coping skills. I must dub her resilient and inspirational. She is strong and tough to overcome abuse, a hurricane, cancer, eyesight deterioration, loss of driver's license and jobs, and if that wasn't horrible enough, child kidnapping and the death of a son. Kudos and accolades to you, Ms. J.! This quote is for you and others who are overcomers.

Behind you, all your memories,

Before you, all your dreams,

Around you, all who love you,

Within you, all you need.

Lili Vaihere[17]

SKILLS TO TRY:

1. Write down in the response section what you learned and what inspired you. What positive things can you put into action?

2. To stop reliving a painful memory—be aware you are ruminating and quickly choose to think about something else. Ask yourself if there is anything you can do about your circumstance. Can you solve something? You can name the painful "thing" or event, such as "Dastardly Defamer," and tell it that it will not cause you harm and tell it to depart. Some counselors teach you to give it time on your terms so you stay in control. Find something to keep yourself busy.

3. Try meditation/prayer. Meditation is more about forming a connection with yourself and gaining awareness. In contrast, prayer is about a connection with God and making your requests known to God. Both reduce stress, decrease depression and anxiety, and help with emotional well-being. It will calm your nervous system so your fight-or-flight response is not activated.

I say this like a broken record. Get support. If you have isolat-

---

17 Lilli Vaihere, *Behind You, All Your Memories. Before You, All Your Dreams. Around You, All Who Love You. Within You, All You Need: 6x9 Inch Lined Journal with Inspirational Quotes.* (Independently Published, 2019).

ed yourself, don't do it alone; at least allow one trusted person in. More would be better. If you are a survivor of abuse, you may have trouble with trust. That is understandable. People who care normally are very good at offering comfort, wisdom/common sense, and practical help, and will help you get your confidence back so you feel you are in control. Unconditional support from someone who will be there for you is vital.

There are resources out there that will help you develop a safety plan. Look for the resources. The number below is one of those resources. The domestic violence hotline is 800–799–7233.

"I will exalt you, O Lord, for You lifted me out of the depths and did not let my enemies gloat over me. O Lord, my God, I called to You for help and you healed me. O Lord, you brought me up from the grave; You spared me from going down into the pit" (Psalm 30:1–3, NIV).

It seems like the psalmist could be close to death as the grave is mentioned. There were very low points and the potential of enemies taking over when there was vulnerability, despair, and weakness. This person (likely David) called on God. He gave Him praise for the rescue as death seemed to be breathing down his neck. God was present when there were bad times as well, and He brought healing. Sadness has turned to joy. This tells me it is possible for restoration from trauma. How? With God, all things are possible. It could be an outright miracle, but more likely, the healing comes one step at a time as you let God have the wounds and hurt places. It's a work in progress.

My side note is this: We have things that happen that feel like we cannot overcome them. Health issues, bills that can't get paid, or Daxton Dastardly has inflicted enough anguish that death would be welcome. God comes through. It's His nature to see to it that His children are taken care of. To understand the pain of trials would take a whole book, but don't give up. Ask, cry out in prayer, and believe!

RESPONSE:

I AM LOOKING
FOR A WARRIOR

What does that mean? Where are you looking and why? A warrior is a person who shows or has shown great valor, courage, or aggressiveness. It can also mean a person engaged in some kind of struggle or conflict.[18] My word would be a trooper or fighter. The thing is, we can all be warriors as we all have some kind of struggle or conflict to engage in. And we don't have to look for a warrior. Just look inside of you. Inside of you is a tough cookie and a survivor. Let me try and bring that characteristic out a bit more.

Carol Pearson, PhD, wrote an article for *Psychology Today*,[19] where she reports warriors generally are associated with two kinds of courage: 1. The ability to fight to protect themselves and 2. Setting goals and developing the strength and skills to accomplish them. She adds, "If we do not have enough access to the Warrior archetype, we may let other people push us around, lack direction, or fail to achieve our goals because we do not persist." Persist, we must.

Because you may have had trauma that interrupted your growth

---

18 Merriam-Webster.com Dictionary, s.v. "warrior," accessed September 3, 2023, https://www.merriam-webster.com/dictionary/warrior.
19 Pearson , Carol S. *"Are You a Warrior? And If So, What Kind?" Psychology Today,* April 23, 2018. https://www.psychologytoday.com/intl/blog/the-hero-within/201804/are-you-warrior-and-if-so-what-kind.

and goals, here are some traits to work on to become the person you want to be. Yes, there are battle scars. Scars tell a story, and that may be what another person needs to hear so they can be not just survivors but warriors and thrivers. The person who has a warrior mentality has confidence and strength and is assertive and disciplined. The warrior does not quit. That's you, not quitting on yourself, not quitting on your family, and not quitting on life in spite of the junk it has thrown your way. It will take you having faith in yourself. It will take you defending your nest (family and home). It will also be you taking a risk and being willing to fail but getting back up.

See if you like this quote/creed by Spartan warriors:[20]

> *I am on a never-ending journey to becoming better today than yesterday, every day.*
>
> *I will always find ways to overcome any obstacles that challenge me.*
>
> *I will not condone fear. It is self-created. And I can remove it.*
>
> *I will lead and inspire others to live their lives more fully every day.*
>
> *There is always a way, and I will make it so.*

Maybe you have been ignored, diminished, talked down to, or abused and felt like you had no or little value. Remember, you can develop a warrior spirit. All battles are internal and external. The internal is what you say to yourself, and the external is what's out there that is quite tough, like how to stay afloat and not sink. The number one characteristic to work on right now to be a warrior is courage.

---

20 "Spartan Warrior Poster Motivational Inspiration." Etsy. https://www.etsy.com/es/listing/1036940109/cartel-de-guerrero-espartano-cartel-de

That is the courage to work on where life went wrong, where the things that happened to you have caused you to feel the opposite of an overcomer, and you lost your passion and purpose. Here's to you getting it back. Comeback, rally, rebound, revive, resurrect, triumph, restore or rejuvenate. You pick your warrior word or phrase. One of my phrases is, "Not happening, devil." I tell myself I may be sweet, but I am very strong.

Do you think of Jesus as the little baby born in a manger, growing up with the greatest high calling, ministering as a man but as the Son of God, dying on the cross, or coming again on a horse? I can think the Lord is all of that, but I can see Him as a warrior as well. Exodus 15:3 (NIV) says, "The Lord is a warrior; The Lord is His name." That means He is the captain of the Lord's hosts, the leader and commander of His people. He has the power to fight and be the victor over His enemies. He is sovereign and supreme, ruling in heaven and in the events of people on earth. Add a visual picture and hang onto the word victor.

Proverbs 21:31 (NIV) says, "The horse is made ready for the day of battle, but victory rests with the Lord." This most likely means that we need to use all reasonable means to protect ourselves and be victorious, but God does the rest. A horse that goes into battle needs to be fed and watered, trained, disciplined, and obedient to its master. Sounds like a spiritual lesson for us.

The story of the Trojan horse has an interesting point. Troy was a city on the coast of Turkey across the sea from the Greek city of Sparta. Troy had a very tall, thick wall that kept the inhabitants inside safe. For ten years, Troy had been under siege. However, one day, a warrior and general named Odysseus had a brilliant idea to build a giant wooden horse and leave it outside the gate of Troy. The army pretended that they were leaving and hoped the people of Troy would think the horse was a gift. As the Trojan people watched the Greeks leave by ship, they opened their protective gate and pulled the horse inside. Under the guise of night, Greek soldiers jumped out of the horse and opened the gates for their awaiting army to attack the Trojans. The result was the end of the Trojan War.

An expression became of that event: "Beware the Greeks bearing gifts." It is a warning against possible deception. What deception? Just like the Greeks were clever enough to sneak their way into a fortified area by using a giant horse, so is our enemy Satan sneaky enough to get in to deceive us. He does not want you to believe you are a warrior but that you are defeated. The opposite is true. He is the defeated foe. Particularly because there have been some deep hurts and possibly life has happened rather cruelly that it makes a person feel vulnerable to the enemy's attacks.

So, first, be aware of his schemes. Like the Trojan horse that was just outside the gate waiting for an opening, there are likewise devils around everywhere waiting for an opportunity to deceive you. Watch those lies he throws out to keep people from seeing and hearing the Gospel. The devil loves it when he can get people to believe that God is not real and does not love them. He will do a good job of trying to convince you that God is not good, especially if you have been through the hurt with Burt and the pain with Blaine. He may even be so good at trying to convince a person that God does not exist and, therefore, go and do their own thing without consequence, sin away. Or he may just try and convince you of his lies, and they will be subtle. You know he can make something evil look like it's the best thing since a double chocolate sundae. Harboring bitterness and unforgiveness gives the devil the right to enter into your life. Yikes, if you allow this, it makes for easy access to be deceived. If you are lacking in faith, then the possibility is strong; you can fall into his trap of deception as you have not built yourself up.

So, here's the scoop: Satan can steal, kill, destroy, capture, hinder, corrupt, harass, smite, persecute, tempt, slander, confuse, and sift you. So, after that gloom and doom, be aware of his schemes, put on the full armor of God, submit to God, be alert, and resist him. Remember you have an advocate, Jesus Christ, who always wins His wars and will see you through to winning your battles. It may not be an easy road, but the road leads to victory as you stand firm. Albert Einstein said that life is like riding a bicycle; to keep your balance, you must keep moving.

By the way, that Trojan horse was described as ten feet wide, twenty-five feet tall, and almost eight feet in length. Satan will try and appear large and in charge. Get this: there were warriors in the horse. You have a warrior in you who is the Lord if you invite Him in, who runs the universe and holds it all together. You have warrior friends also, so don't forget to use them to war with you. David killed the bear and the lion, and he killed huge Goliath, his biggest enemy, because God was with him and gave him ideas, wisdom, strength, and stamina.

"When God's warrior goes down on their knees, the battle is not over. It has just begun."[21]

Unknown

"I do what I do because it is the right thing to do. I am a warrior, and it is the way of the warrior to fight superior odds."

Paul Watson

"A true warrior, like tea, shows his strength in hot water."

Warrior Quotes[22]

21 praiseJesustoday.com
22 *"QUOTATION #127573."* Quotery. Accessed September 14, 2023. https://www.quotery.com/

SKILLS TO TRY:

1. Allow time to grieve and time to adjust. But then, get up and on with life as you want to carve it out.

2. It is very important not to isolate yourself. Be with healthy, safe, and caring people. A positive support system will be a source of strength to you and help you on your road to trusting again. They also may be helpful with practical things.

3. Absolutely no put-downs to yourself. As you are avoiding self-criticism, make sure you are respecting yourself and being kind to yourself.

4. Apply stress management techniques. My first book, *Stuff Your Fanny Pack with Coping Skills*, is full of stress management strategies.

5. Everyone needs goals. Be realistic and make them achievable. Never let the tough places in life keep you from pursuing what is in your heart. Get creative.

6. Make this the beginning of developing you. Recognize your strengths and improve your relationships.

7. Lack of courage often comes from fear. What steps can you take, even if baby steps, to be proactive to reduce and then eliminate your fears?

8. Remember the warrior mentality. Be your own hero. Your courage is really there; it could be hidden due to the trauma. Maybe all you could do at that time was try and protect yourself. Tell yourself you have the ability to start over, and you will. The Terminator said, "I'll be

quotes/true-warrior-like-tea-shows.

back."[23] Be back in the game, however tough it was to play.

9. If you have been feeling overwhelmed, then breathe and step away from what is causing you such anxiety. Stepping away will give your brain time to see what you can do differently. You are making positive life changes to manage life better now. Even though it seems like your past is never really past, remind yourself that it is history and you are working on a new, happier, more positive, courageous way to live. Feeling overwhelmed and anxious does not have to last. Your past may cause you to be predisposed to depression and anxiety. Be patient. Take a look back to see how far you have come, then keep moving ahead.

10. You will need to develop self-confidence. That translates to being a bit vulnerable and taking risks. Be smart about it, though. What risks should you take? What risks are not a good idea at this time?

11. There will always be obstacles. What are your obstacles? Make a plan for each obstacle. If you consult with trusted family and friends, they just may tell you what you want to do is a good idea and help you. Or at least they are there to bounce things off of.

12. In case you have allowed a "Trojan horse" in your home, remember the formula: to put on your armor, be aware of the devil's schemes, submit to God, be alert, and resist him. Don't forget to use Scripture and prayer. I have always believed, especially when the stakes are high, to get others to hold you up and pray for you and yours.

---

23 Cameron, James. Terminator. 1984. Los Angeles, CA: Orion Pictures.

13. Believe in yourself. Love yourself. Maybe you can even love your scars as they represent something to you that was difficult, but also you overcame it. Get control of any negative, self-defeating thoughts. If you believe in yourself, you will likely take better care of yourself and make better decisions. A warrior feels like they can accomplish whatever they want to. What can you say to yourself to increase that belief?

"Do not be afraid; you will not suffer shame. Do not fear disgrace; you will not be humiliated" (Isaiah 54:4a, NIV).

The Jewish people were in bondage in Egypt, and they had extreme trials, but ahead of them was a future full of hope. They were instructed to forget the shame of their youth as abundance would come. Do not fear. It may seem impossible not to have fear, disgrace, and not be humiliated. After all, some bad things have happened. You are to look ahead at the Lord, who makes things right.

RESPONSE:

_____

_____

_____

_____

_____

_____

_____

_____

_____

_____

_____

_____

_____

_____

_____

_____

_____

_____

_____

_____

_____

_____

_____

THE PHOENIX

I am writing about the phoenix because it is a symbol of hope and resilience. It also symbolizes renewal or to be rebuilt. I want that for you. This bird is in Greek mythology. There is much to learn from it that you can apply to yourself. The phoenix can rise from the ashes of its predicament. To rise from the ashes means to emerge from a catastrophe stronger, smarter, and more powerful.[24] Now that says empowered all over it. Let's discuss how to get you on that journey to wholeness.

I would never be so insensitive as to assume that recovery after trauma is quick. Your life has forever been changed, but it does not have to all be negative and ashes. It is definitely a process, and you go at your own pace. With that being said, skills to travel on that journey are helpful.

Isaiah 61:2b–3 states the Lord wants to comfort all who mourn, provide for those who grieve, and bestow on them a crown of beauty instead of ashes, the oil of gladness instead of mourning, and a garment of praise instead of a spirit of despair. What good news. But, if that is not your reality now, stay tuned, as God is not done.

An important thing to get to empowerment is to understand why you need this. Empowerment, according to the Oxford Languages Dictionary, means the process of becoming stronger and

---

24 grammerist.com

more confident, especially in controlling one's life and claiming one's rights.[25] It will help you make positive decisions to achieve your goals. Self-empowerment would mean you make choices to get control of your life back. It will help you live to your fullest and help you believe in yourself and that tomorrow can get better.

There are words that can be very beneficial if one begins to latch onto them. This is most helpful as your brain may need a bit of reprogramming from what trauma has done. Also, there is the likelihood that if you were involved in intimate partner violence (IPV), you were assaulted not only physically but verbally. Pick your favorites from this list of words to keep in your vocabulary to build yourself up:

strength	tenacity	fortitude	power
self-sufficient	self-determined	persistent	grit
backbone	balance	brave	capable
thriving	peace	purpose	nurture
improvement	growing	learning	calm
confident	conquer	grateful	fearless
happy	joyful	release	grace
spiritual	laughing	simplify	safe
positive	hopeful	breathe	healing
acceptance	value	courage	heart
admiration	blessed	breakthrough	self-preservation

Now hang onto these self-empowering statements:

1. I am safe.

2. I am in control.

3. I am worthy of respect.

25 "Empowerment." empowerment noun—Definition, pictures, pronunciation and usage notes | Oxford Advanced Learner's Dictionary at OxfordLearners-Dictionaries.com. Accessed September 3, 2023. https://www.oxfordlearners-dictionaries.com/definition/english/empowerment.

4. I will not let my past control my future.

5. I am enough.

6. I am capable of making good decisions.

7. God is always with me.

8. What happened does not define me.

9. It was not my fault.

10. I am not a mistake.

11. I will treat myself with kindness.

12. I will ask for help when I need to.

13. I deserve to be loved.

14. I am valuable.

15. I will accept compliments.

16. I am doing the best I can.

17. My feelings count.

18. I can do wonderful things.

Rahab in Joshua 2 in the Bible was an example of a phoenix-type individual as she rose from the ashes as a prostitute who became a heroine. Joshua had sent two men as spies to Jericho to get some intel on how to take Jericho, a fortified and evil city. The king of Jericho found out and wanted them hunted down. Rahab had them in her home, had to lie to the king about their whereabouts, then rose to the occasion and turned her rooftop into a hiding place. The unusual circumstance was she was an enemy of the spies, and she was known as an immoral woman. She helped them escape through a window and suggested they hide in the hills for three days. Her request for the kindness she offered for their getaway was to keep her family safe when they returned to take over Jericho.

One who was a harlot is now listed in Hebrews 11:31 as a hero of faith. How can that be? She had faith and put her trust in God. She came to believe in the God of the spies. She believed that the God of Israel is God in heaven above and on earth below (Joshua 2:11). Rahab took a risk. She had courage. She knew what was about to happen, but she was not selfish. She could have gotten out, but she made sure her family would be able to escape.

Think about this: It does not matter if you are considered lowly, poor, or of an unprincipled reputation. The Lord wants you saved, and He wants to intervene in all of your life. His divine providence was at work for the people in Israel, for Rahab and her family. His sovereign guidance and control are at work for us as well.

For someone to be a risk taker, they have to be willing to go outside of their comfort zone and not let fear stop them. It needs to be for a positive or healthy goal. Danger could be involved, such as Rahab risking her life. If you have been in a difficult or intolerable situation, then taking a risk and making a change would require you to manage uncertainty. Decisions have to be made to make your needed changes, so be wise and look at all angles. Calculate the risk. Rahab was fearless but not impulsive. Her will was strengthened to keep on keeping on. Again, with empowerment— it will keep you going and moving out to a more positive life. That life will not just knock on your door; you have to go after it. Do not be afraid if there are setbacks.

SKILLS TO TRY:

1. There are forty-four words that are empowering in the list above. Take them one by one and make a sentence

that is positive about yourself. For instance, "I am confident good things are ahead for me" or "I will nurture myself every day."

2. From the list of empowering statements, speak each one to yourself and speak it over yourself until it is reality. Then, continue to use your favorites every day.

3. Look at what you already coped with. Look at what you were able to withstand. Look at the changes you have made. You didn't go under. You went over, around, or through.

4. Avoid seeing your circumstance as insurmountable. Start making goals to problem-solve everything happening currently.

5. As tough as this is to hear, can you find meaning in what you are going through? Can you begin a self-discovery of finding your purpose?

6. Change is constant. Try embracing it rather than fighting against it.

7. Get your voice back. Say what you need and go after it. Say it assertively, not with disrespect, as others will tune you out.

8. It is important to have a safe physical outlet so you can release the feelings regarding the trauma.

9. I cannot say enough about finding safe and stable connections. It is a gift you give to yourself. Make the positive relationship reciprocal.

10. Know your strengths and weaknesses.

11. If you have circumstances where you need divine in-

tervention, then ask God to take over. His love, mercy, and protection will see you through. Be sure to listen for how He may need you to cooperate with His plan. Rahab cooperated.

12. Having examined all the information about being like a phoenix and rising from your ashes stronger and smarter. Rahab was living a life where her lifestyle was looked down on, but she triumphed and saved herself and saw to it that others were saved. Consider what needs to be done in your situation. Personalize it for you and yours that are affected, such as your children. Write down what you want and need and how you will go after it. It would be good to consult trusted others who may be needed in your plan and can be a resource.

Okay, Phillip Phoenix and Phyllis Phoenix, go get your power back. Move in the direction of feeling competent.

"My dark days made me strong. Or maybe I already was strong, and they made me prove it."

Emery Lord

Do not fret because of evil men or be envious of those who do wrong; for like the grass they will soon wither, like green plants they will soon die away. Trust in the Lord and do good; dwell in the land and enjoy safe pasture. Delight yourself in the Lord and He will give you the desires of your heart.

Psalm 37:1–4 (NIV)

When one is traumatized, it appears that the evil doers come across as doing well. However, that so-called power or favor is fleeting. It says it will be cut down, and it will wither. Instead of being upset at those who do evil, trust in the Lord instead. Here is the formula: trust and delight in Him, and He gives us the desires of our hearts that line up with His will. Being safe, happy, and healthy would be in that category.

RESPONSE:

_____

_____

_____

_____

_____

_____

_____

_____

_____

_____

_____

_____

_____

_____

_____

_____

_____

_____

A DAZZLING TRAUMA

Try and guess this. What is beautiful but can smell weird? What glows and can whistle? What is sporadic but can be gone in seconds? The answer is fireworks. I am putting this in a trauma lesson to make a comparison between anxiety and post-traumatic stress. Since fireworks are combustible, they make loud noises, some of which can sound like a gun going off. They can whistle, whizz, pop, crack, screech, and go boom at the same time they display their beauty. They may smell of sulfur.

Let me tell you about Annie's trauma. I have a rescue border collie named Annie. She came from a hoarder. She came to me already skittish as she had lived in a cage for two and a half years to breed her in a home where forty other dogs were. I expect she never had it quiet. She was so grateful to be rescued that she kept her eye on me rather constantly. We were trying to get her not to be so anxious, and then came the holidays, where fireworks were used to celebrate. Annie would hide under the desk, under a coffee table, in a closet, or between the wall and the toilet and shake. We tried turning the television up and the dryer on to drown out the boom noise. I have not medicated her as I am trying other things. Forget about her going out for potty before bed. She could not do it. She was traumatized. My two previous dogs were equally frightened.

Ray Brown, host of the "Talkin' Birds" podcast, reports that fireworks spook birds so badly that they actually panic. To make it worse, they hear the loud noise at night, and they leave their roost/nests, which may have eggs or babies, and the birds can't see where they are going. He adds that they crash, and their nest is left open for predators. Being a nature lover, I can only imagine that birds and squirrels and other critters of mother nature could be happily sleeping and then kaboom. Aah, poor things. I feel bad about the case scenario.

In case you are wondering, I used to love to take my children to fireworks displays, but I will not buy them anymore due to the trauma they cause to pets, livestock, wildlife, and those who struggle with post-traumatic stress. Some towns have adopted the practice of laser shows instead, which I say is a big kudos to the management of those towns. Some people can buy low-noise pyrotechnics. I am not a hater, so don't write me about it. I just prefer not to scare the pets, vets, and critters in the neighborhood.

So, compare the fireworks to what it might feel like to someone who has post-traumatic stress (PTS), post-traumatic stress disorder (PTSD), or anxiety. Small things upset the person who has been through traumatic events, so loud noises that suddenly surprise them would for sure. A person may have an idea that at certain times and holidays, they could be exposed to certain noises, but the survivor of trauma can suddenly be triggered and feel overwhelmed by a noise, a place, a person, objects, or even a smell. Flashbacks can occur due to "re-experiencing" a trauma. Flashbacks are defined as frequent intrusive recollections of the traumatic event and acting or feeling as though it were happening again. People can feel like they are actually in the time, place, and location again. Nightmares can be a problem as they disrupt sleep and life in general. The flashback is like fireworks, as it can come on suddenly. The smoke from fireworks can remind a person of being in a war zone, burning skin, going into a burning building, being a burn victim, or working with burn victims.

Annie did what is called avoidance and isolation as she was afraid. Somewhere in her dog brain, she knew to hide as she "wanted to survive." It is the same for the human survivor. The idea of avoidance is to avoid contact with the triggers for anxiety, fear, or memories or thoughts. The isolation part is in the trauma survivor's mind as self-preservation. The thought is if you are left alone, you are less likely to be triggered. Sometimes, those who have trouble dealing with their feelings prefer to isolate. They also feel like other people could never understand the horrors they went through. Isolation can lead to depression, and depression can lead to suicidal ideation. We are meant to be interconnected with one another and to be connected to God.

A great resource I read about came from Chris Adsit, an author, veteran, and reverend. He wrote *The Combat Trauma and Healing Manual*.[26] He stated, "Okay, the crisis is over now. I survived. What happened wasn't pretty, but the score ended up me—1, the grave—0. So, why can't I move on? Why do I keep reliving what happened?" He adds that if the trauma was particularly violent or life-threatening or there were multiple episodes, the brain is likely stuck in crisis-alert mode. He calls it "PTSD persistence."

Chris Adsit gives this example worthy to be shared. Think of it in terms of walking across a frozen lake. Suddenly, you hear a loud pop, and you notice the ice is cracking under your feet. You instantly freeze. Your arms reflexively shoot out from your sides for balance, and your feet spread wide to distribute your weight. Your muscles are now tight, your shoulders are hunched up, and your eyes are the size of softballs, and you begin to take very small, careful steps back the way you came. After about twenty yards, you're beyond where the cracks were. Do you think you'd

---

26 Christopher B. Adsit, *The Combat Trauma Healing Manual: Christ-centered Solutions for Combat Trauma.* (CreateSpace Independent Publishing Platform, 2007).

go bounding merrily the rest of the way to shore? You'd probably remain on high alert the rest of the way because you are now aware that the ice could give away beneath you at any time. After a traumatic event, your brain knows that it just had an incredibly close call, and it is determined to be ready to react if the danger comes by again. Good idea—except it gets stuck in that mode, which is what PTSD essentially is.

Before I give you skills, let's look at how post-traumatic stress is defined. Dr. James Bender from the Deployment Health Center defines it as a common and normal response to experiencing a traumatic or stressful event. Pretty much everyone who has experienced a frightening event will have some post-traumatic stress.

Dr. Bender continues that if you're experiencing post-traumatic stress, your heart may race, your hands shake, and you may sweat or feel afraid and nervous. After the stress event, you might avoid or be leery of engaging in that activity again, you may have a bad dream about the event you just experienced, or you may feel nervous in a situation that reminds you of the unpleasant event. Although they can be momentarily intense, symptoms of post-traumatic stress usually subside a few days after the event and won't cause any prolonged meaningful interference with your life. One positive outcome of experiencing post-traumatic stress may be that you behave more carefully in a potentially dangerous situation in the future. It is not a mental illness.

On the other hand, post-traumatic stress disorder, according to the Diagnostic and Statistical Manual of Mental Disorders (DSM-5),[27] is defined as an intense or prolonged psychological distress at exposure to internal or external cues that symbolize or resemble an aspect of the traumatic event(s). Symptoms would include four categories: intrusion (repeated, involuntary memories; distress-

---

[27] Diagnostic and Statistical Manual of Mental Disorders (5th ed.; DSM–5; American Psychiatric Association, 2013).

ing dreams, or flashbacks), avoidance (avoiding reminders of the traumatic event), negative changes in thought and mood (distorted beliefs, fear, guilt, shame, and lack of happiness) and changes in arousal and reactivity (being angry, behaving recklessly, hypervigilant, easily startled, or trouble sleeping or concentrating). The clinical definition is an anxiety disorder that develops in reaction to physical injury or severe mental or emotional distress.

According to psychiatry.com, PTSD can occur in all people of any ethnicity, nationality, or culture and at any age. An estimated one in eleven people will be diagnosed with PTSD in their lifetime. The National Center for PTSD in the US reports there are 12 million adults in the US with PTSD. They divide that up as 8 out of 100 women develop PTSD sometime in their lives, and about 4 out of 100 men. The US Department of Veteran Affairs states the prevalence of PTSD for veterans depends on war zone deployment, training accidents, and military sexual trauma.

The apostle Paul is a study in contrasts. On the one hand, he said in 2 Corinthians 1:8–9 that he was under great pressure beyond his ability to endure to the point that he despaired even of life and felt the sentence of death. Even the best Christians who are walking solidly with the Lord can be discouraged. Never beat yourself up. Paul had a lot happening, from great persecution, pain, and severe criticism, and he does not tell what had him so overwhelmed that he thought it was the end. Trouble hit him hard, and it does for us today. You may feel like Diane Dilemma or Turner Turbulent. We share the trials that Christ had. On the flip side, we can share the comfort that was His as well. True comfort has a spiritual source. The comfort may come in the form of His presence, His deliverance, something in the Word that ministers to us, or a person who comes along in our time of distress. Paul came to the conclusion that we should not trust in our own strength but in God. Paul's confidence did return with his proclamation that since God could raise

Christ from the dead, He could raise him from what felt like death.

Paul also had a "thorn in the flesh" (2 Corinthians 12:7–8). It never went away. It could be the same for some people who have and will suffer with their condition for the rest of their lives. With that being said, one can minimize the symptoms and do some things so life can still be full. Paul did hang onto hope. Try and see your circumstances through the Lord's perspective. Paul's thorn camped out in, on, or near him to the end of his days. God reassured him that His grace was sufficient to meet his challenges. God's grace defined is His divine influence that operates in and through and for us; His kindness, favor, love, and mercy are just a part of that. It shows up in His divine providence (all things that occur are under His sovereign guidance and control), gift of salvation, rescue, deliverance, and favor we don't deserve.

Bad things happen, and it feels like they go on and on like a hail storm that plummets. I read about what was called "gorilla hail," which was hail the size of a grapefruit or baseball. That was a term given by a meteorologist named Reed Timmer. Now, if that was coming down on me or my possessions, there is going to be some hurt, cracks, dents, and something broken. In comparison, trials and the kind of events that make a person want to quit on life or feel like their "thorns" will last forever need to remember God's presence is sufficient to meet all challenges. During my many years of tough life things, I told the Lord I knew He was aware of me; therefore, I could believe He was at work on and behind the scenes.

SKILLS TO TRY:

1. 1. So, there are fireworks that could be caused by other people, knowingly or unknowingly. There are cracks in your walk, thorns in the flesh, or gorilla hail. That's the

big ball of hard stuff. Obviously, the hail can be huge, like trauma, or smaller, like hurts. Consider trying therapy and possibly medication to ease the severity of the symptoms. Social support is big. Getting help will require that you lay aside your beliefs about asking. It does not, I repeat, does not make you incompetent or weak. Some parts of your life have been out of control, but being overly independent is not working, and it will not serve you well in the present or future. Maybe you have shut down emotionally, and it is understandable you have used that to cope and feel safe, but it will not help you heal. Maybe your defenses are up, and a wall surrounds you, but it is avoidance, and it will not help you get back to enjoyment of life. Yes, I said enjoy-ment. Little by little, you do what you can and take up doing things you enjoy and being with people you love.

2.   2. Don't get caught up in the perception of "normal." I mean, you want to find that for yourself, and you can't tell if others think you are normal or not. You can't give this concern as it will cause you to feel over-whelmed and vigilant. Be you doing your best to walk on your ice as described above. Get to solid ground— your strong life. Down deep inside, your mind knows you heard, smelled, touched, and witnessed the worst of life: the unimaginable. People will not understand unless they went through it themselves. But you can explain if you want to and if you can, as the language area of the brain has been affected. You can explain why you won't go to the fireworks display, go on a boat or helicopter, or even an amusement park ride, or help a stranger who may be holding something wrapped. You can explain why a certain road has too many ob-stacles on the side of the road that trigger your memory

of being ambushed or why a certain area of town is too much of a reminder of a fire or bombing.

Trauma is deep in the brain. The trigger is like hail coming down, and you are aroused, and when it is the thorn in the flesh, you are numb and avoiding, or maybe you are just maintaining. Either way, please gift yourself with therapy to learn some skills and where you will get support and encouragement. You are not likely to ever erase the trauma from the brain, but you can get some control back by coming to terms with it and learning skills. To go it alone will be detrimental. Isolation is your cracked ice.

3. Connect spiritually. Connect with what you perceive God to be, connect with His inspired word, and be part of a body of believers who can offer care, support, and possible resources. Be part of the activities. Being part of a body of believers will help you be involved with others who may be mature, and you can learn from them as well as develop from the teaching. The Lord will also get his due worship when there is participation in the music. I just must say to never forget the fact that He brings an arsenal of hope, help, encouragement, mercy, grace, and provision.

"And the God of all grace, who called you to His eternal glory in Christ, after you have suffered a little while, will Himself restore you and make you strong, firm and steadfast" (1 Peter 5:10, NIV).

Did you read it says "will Himself"? God Himself is going to do it. That has power and love all over it. He will establish us, restore, mend, strengthen, and settle us. That has a wow factor. All the fragmented pieces of our lives can be mended. It says after a while, so hang in there. He can make the impossible possible.

RESPONSE:

IT'S KIND OF LIKE A DEVIL

Are you wondering what is kind of like a devil? Okay, let's talk about what animal is very aggressive; it is actually savage and has an exceedingly powerful bite with bone-crushing jaws. It can easily fly into a rage. I am going to say it is an opportunist and a formidable foe. This animal can even get a facial tumor disease from fighting and mating. It also has an ear-splitting shriek. Any guess? It is the Tasmanian devil.

The comparison is to complex post-traumatic stress (C-PTSD) as it will feel like a Tasmanian devil because it creates such trauma. C-PTSD is prolonged, repeated, and ongoing. Examples are childhood abuse or trauma, physical abuse, emotional abuse, sexual abuse or neglect. It is powerful, aggressive, and savage to have to endure, and it feels like it will not let up. That Tasmanian devil will not let up until it has eaten the bone, hair, and all of the carcass. C-PTSD is brutal. It is also an opportunist as it exploits one's situation, trying to gain an advantage over the person. It, too, is disturbing and dreadful like an enemy. The Tasmanian devil's facial tumor disease causes tumors that grow rapidly around the head and neck, which causes the animal not to be able to eat; thus, death usually occurs within six months of onset. I cannot compare C-PTSD to that, but I can say it eats away at the core of your being.

It changes the brain. Especially if a child has C-PTSD, their brain has not fully developed.

The National Foundation to End Child Abuse and Neglect (ENDCAN) wrote an article[28] with this information: "The brain and body are still developing in childhood and are strongly affected by stressors like neglect or other abuse. C-PTSD often occurs before a child's cognitive abilities and sense of self have fully developed, affecting how the brain and communication systems will eventually develop. When children have C-PTSD, their brains learn to constantly assume and respond to minor signs of a possible threat. Adrenaline and cortisol continuously flood the body as a result. Since fighting back or running away is rarely an option, the child will instead shut down, dissociate, and freeze. However, adrenalin and cortisol continue throughout the body, affecting the immune and digestive systems and possibly causing psychosomatic symptoms."

It helps to have information from the same source, ENDCAN, pertaining to how C-PTSD affects adulthood. Because children rarely understand that their body's response is a reaction to chronic trauma, the behavior patterns they develop follow them into adulthood, even when their environment seems relatively safe. Their stress response is hyperactive and causes an increase in adrenaline and cortisol at the slightest perceived threat. The result can be repressed memories of the event, flashbacks, and multiple problems in relationships and the workplace. In some instances, it can cause individuals to try and override the stress response by indulging in high levels of drugs, alcohol, spending, sex, and working. Others may inadvertently try to recreate the traumatic childhood event through behaviors or relationships either because it is familiar or because they are trying to fix it. Adult survivors of C-PTSD can experience problems regulating their emotions, leading to severe

28 ENDCAN (2022) *Complex PTSD and Childhood Trauma, ENDCAN.* Available at: https://endcan.org/2022/06/13/complex-ptsd-and-childhood-trauma/ (Accessed: 14 September 2023).

depression, suicidal thoughts, or problems controlling their anger. They may also view themselves as being different from others, causing feelings of detachment, helplessness, shame, and guilt.

If you have been through any kind of trauma, it is imperative to keep hope. Hope means you keep your mind on track for a positive outcome. You desire something to happen. Keeping hope will inspire you and motivate you to move into a better future.

Basically, complex PTSD is post-traumatic stress disorder in a severe form. The person suffering will have difficulty with their traumatic memories being over-activated; therefore, they may startle easily, can't sleep well, and seem to be on guard a lot. There could be episodes of anger and aggressive behavior. The personality of the sufferer changes to the point that trust becomes a big problem, and intimacy will suffer. Forget about self-esteem, as feelings of worthlessness, shame, and guilt are heavy. In trying to control the emotional roller coaster, the result can be serious depression and suicidal ideation. The traumatized individual may dissociate, which means the person feels disconnected from their thoughts, feelings, memories, and surroundings. This can also cause a person to feel numb, have an altered sense of time, forget things, and have severe flashbacks that seem real. Essentially, your mind is trying to help you so you don't experience the full and intense experience you had.

Professor Andreas Maercker and other researchers from Germany, using the results from 2,500 adults, report that the complex form of PTSD was most present in people who had experienced sexual abuse in childhood or repeated sexual assaults as adolescents or adults.[29] That is not all, as repeated witnessing violence or abuse, being forced into prostitution, torture, capture, accidents,

---

29 University of Zurich. *"0.5 percent of the population suffer from severe psychological trauma."* ScienceDaily. www.sciencedaily.com/releases/2018/01/180131124623.htm (accessed September 14, 2023).

natural disasters, or being a prisoner of war can cause complex PTSD.

Journey of Smiley[30] reports some great quotes. Take them into your brain and heart like a healing elixir:

> *"Be gentle with yourself. You are doing the best you can."*
>
> **Paulo Coelho**

> *"Do not rush, for God's secret is patience. Everything that is meant to be will come at a designated time."*
>
> **Leon Brown**

> *"Forgiveness is no longer an option but a necessity for healing."*
>
> **Caroline Myss**

> *"It's okay to not be okay, but it is not okay to stay that way."*
>
> **Perry Noble**

> *"No one can listen to your body for you...To grow and heal, you have to take responsibility for listening to it yourself."*
>
> **Jon Kabot-Zinn**

> *"Healing takes time, and asking for help is a courageous step."*
>
> **Mariska Hargitay**

---

30 Parker, Katy. "Year of Healing: 10 Positive Recovery Quotes." Journeyofsmiley, December 27, 2021. https://journeyofsmiley.com/healing-10-positive-recovery-quotes/.

"Your wound is not your fault, but your healing is your responsibility."

Denise Frohman

SKILLS TO TRY:

1. Complex PTSD is that: complex. I highly recommend being under the care of a licensed practitioner. Several things may be tried, such as cognitive behavioral therapy, which will help with changing negative thoughts and behaviors. Possibly, Eye Movement Desensitization and Reprocessing (EMDR), which uses visual exercises to help with the traumatic events. In combination, a doctor may prescribe medication to help with depression, anxiety, and insomnia. Take a chance and form an alliance so you can begin to rebuild. You carry your trauma every day, so connect with the professionals so you can learn to thrive in spite of it. Thriving is possible even when you don't think so. It means to grow, prosper, be fortunate, or be successful. It also means to work on yourself.

2. Start your day with courage and hope. Don't keep any thoughts of dread. That thinking will only keep gloom and doom hanging out like an outbreak of lice. Find something you have to look forward to in your day. Even if it is simple, like your favorite muffin awaits its demise, and your friend said she needed your help to pick out a new outfit. Coffee or tea and a soothing shower are something to anticipate. If you can keep hope, you will feel more empowered to adjust to your new "normal." First of all, what realistic plans do you want to see that happen? What do you need to do to get some positive things going? What are the things you

can control? What gives you purpose? For example, an important thing for me is that I have told my dog I will try and live past her as she needs me. I have told my sons I want to be at my grandchildren's graduations and weddings. Endure and plunge forward with something you want and need and add doing for another. You know, those acts of kindness that can be small but mean so much.

3. Look at your life as full of possibilities, not full of limitations. That will require some work on your part to exchange negative thinking for hopeful and positive thinking. You probably have low expectations, but take a look and see if there is some tweaking needed. Try optimism in spite of uncertainty. It will feel good. Think innovation, adventure, rebuilding, reworking and reshaping.

The Lord is my shepherd, I shall not be in want. He makes me lie down in green pastures, He leads me beside quiet waters, He restores my soul. He guides me in paths of righteousness for His name's sake. Even though I walk through the valley of the shadow of death, I will fear no evil, for you are with me; your rod and your staff they comfort me.

Psalm 23:1–4 (NIV)

A very famous passage where David is more mature now and he has seen the faithfulness of God. He has experienced the shadow of death. A green pasture is a symbol of rest and peace. Quiet waters would mean it's not raging. It sounds so wonderful, especially when life has been tumultuous. Latch onto the truth here. Make sure you have made the Lord your shepherd. He is in the restoration business. How wonderful for our hurting minds and bodies.

RESPONSE:

_____

_____

_____

_____

_____

_____

_____

_____

_____

_____

_____

_____

_____

_____

_____

_____

_____

_____

_____

_____

_____

ELLIE ELEPHANT HAS A STORY TO TELL

My name is Ellie Elephant. Go with it, please—there are some strong points. When I was a baby, I watched my mother get killed, my father get shot, and his tusks were quickly and brutally cut off of him. The why of all of that is still a mystery. I hurt emotionally. I know what a gun is, and I heard it fired several times. My older brother ran towards the threat. Maybe that was his instinct to show he was large and in charge or to give the rest of us a greater chance to escape. Only some of us escaped. It seemed to me he was trying to protect us. We ran and ran. One elephant fell into a hole that humans dug to capture her. After escaping, we encountered a pack of hyenas who took out my friend. I was in shock. What was left of my dismantled herd experienced drought and hunger. I have been traumatized severely. I miss my family and friends. I still needed my mom, and I feel lost without her. Now, I am an orphan.

It has been two years since that terrible day when cruel poachers killed my family and heartless men injured others in my herd for reasons that will never be understood. I have an excellent memory, and the trauma still haunts me. I have been depressed and anxious. Yes, elephants grieve. I have spent many a day just swaying and rocking to self-soothe. On other days, I can startle easily and feel aggressive. The loss has caused me to miss out on the matriarchal society where I had parents, siblings, friends, and other families who taught me and protected me. There are days I simply don't know what to do, and I can't make a decision. I miss the affection I used to have.

I have post-traumatic stress, much like humans, but I also have an orphan mentality. Maybe you do, too. It makes me feel like people cannot be trusted, and you have only yourself to rely on. There have been days I felt isolated, lonely, and hopeless. I had to grow up quickly and mostly learn to fend for myself without the older generation to lead and guide me. My view of life is generally pessimistic. A lot of times, I feel like withdrawing from humans altogether and other animals. It feels like I don't fit in anywhere.

Even elephants need to learn how to cope. Ellie continues, "Forget I won't, but cope I must! I am an African elephant and could live to be sixty or seventy years old. Staying with this great amount of sadness was not going to be my option. I must go on, and so must you if you have had trauma. That was a conclusion I finally had to come to."

Since elephants are much like humans in their emotions, here are the suggestions by Ellie Elephant that people can learn from.

1. Family life is everything. That includes friend life as well. A person (or animal) doesn't move past a devastating experience very well in isolation. Allow positive people in. That means you give permission for others to be in your life. You allow time and opportunity for connections. You communicate. Elephants have allomothers, which are other elephants who are not the biological mothers but care for the orphaned elephants. For you, that means that, especially if you are young, you can use the support, help, and nurturing of others to fill that need. In a herd, an elephant feels the safety

of being connected, especially if humans have been brutal to them.

2. Elephants have good adapting abilities. They have their sheer size to help with that. They have other bodily features such as a trunk to grasp, ears to flap to keep them cool, wrinkles to keep them cool, and an ability to detect water up to twelve miles away. They can hear from a distance of over five miles away. Those tusks can strip bark from trees, dig in the dirt, and be used as weapons against predators. Their trunk is used to pull branches down and to get water. Elephants have long eyelashes to protect against sand, debris, and dirt. They have a third eyelid which moves vertically to protect them when they are busy feeding and bathing. On the flip side, the trunk is also used to soothe a scared elephant or, in general, to display affection.

So, what skills as humans do we have to adapt to life? How about the ability to walk on two feet, have a useful opposable thumb, and have an intelligent and complex brain? Humans have a strong ability for endurance. We can adapt to severe environments such as extreme cold or intense heat and at high altitudes. Humans can cool themselves by sweating. We can adapt to social environments and read a room, such as whether or not to stay there. And let's not forget that although the brain is amazing, so is the heart. The brain sends signals to the heart to help us survive but also to direct our moods. So, the question is: life has been hard, so what areas do you need to focus on to adapt to your new circumstances so as to move past painful memories?

3. Elephants communicate. Elephants make sounds from their trunks, mouth, forehead, and chest. It may be a click, purr, rumble, squeal, bark, grunt, groan, or trumpet sound. They can produce low-frequency rumbles known as seismic or infrasound, which humans cannot hear. The rumble sends signals through the elephant's feet and into the ground for up to thirty miles away. They are also very tactile, using touch for about everything positive (Elephant Aid International). Most people could do better with this.

After trauma, communication can be tied to trust tissues. Our identity is formed and reshaped by the people whom we trust. Trust is not passive resignation to one's new, altered life. One must forget the naysayers. How do you move on when listening to Wendy Wetblanket or Solomon Sourpuss? Is there any place you are negatively communicating? For example, raising your voice when not necessary, interrupting, overtalking, arguing and always needing to be right, gossiping, and cursing. Examine where you need to improve communication. For example, are you being an active listener, making eye contact, and using appropriate body language?

So, why the big deal about communication and trauma? If you are a survivor, there is a challenge in expressing yourself and understanding others. Concentration is skewed. Talking is difficult because talking about the trauma could involve re-traumatization. Fear comes up because a survivor does not want to be judged, rejected, or even not believed. Pain receptors for social and physical pain are in the same part of the brain. We are wired to need love and acceptance, and when it does not happen, people can choose to avoid it and forgo any communication, thus social isolation. Rejection can equate to retaliation and aggression. Be patient with yourself if you are experiencing aggression, hypervigilance, or withdrawal.

Trust can be reestablished by the giving and receiving of respect and being transparent with your communication. Also, empathy is a big deal. Don't think there is something wrong with you, but rather, something has happened to you. It's a better mindset and respectful. Keep that thought when dealing with other trauma survivors. It also helps a person have dignity.

4. Elephants are resourceful. They love each other very much. They will help each other, express empathy for one another, and be kind, caring, and sensitive to each other. They show compassion. Elephants mourn when they lose one in their herd. They will caress the deceased elephant and even have a moment of silence. They demonstrate how they bury their dead by covering them with dirt, leaves, and branches. They toss dust onto wounded elephants. They do everything to help their own if another has fallen into a hole or mud pit.

Their resourcefulness is also found in their problem-solving skills and their innate ability to preserve their habitats, therefore helping the ecosystem. Modifying their environment is something we can learn from. The ways they have learned to survive are ingenious, and in doing this, they make a way for smaller animals to survive.

Now, back to us human beings. Resourcefulness means the ability and creativity to cope with difficult situations or unusual problems. It is about problem-solving and getting things done in the face of obstacles and constraints. This would require determination and not giving up. It is not letting life's challenges stop you. Resourceful people find ways to adapt to the situation or environment. The elephant family system has elders who teach the younger ones. For people, isn't that a positive way to move forward and pay forward? Besides, it will feel good to help others. Elephants know when to ask for help. Any pride would have to go so humans can ask for help.

SKILLS TO TRY:

1. So, there you have the elephant life as it could parallel to lessons learned. Ellie was so traumatized, and yet, in time, she realized she needed to move forward by developing more positive relationships, adapting, communicating, and being resourceful. What have you learned, and where do you need to make changes?

2. Remember, to an elephant, a trunk is practical and most useful. It is used to "give a hug" and hold another close. Where can you get your emotional and physical needs met without putting yourself at risk? Please give this some serious consideration as we have these needs, but I want you to be safe and with the right "trunk" people.

"I will not leave you as orphans; I will come to you" (John 14:18, NIV).

Jesus does not want anyone to be left as an orphan. The disciples are nervous, so the Lord is reassuring them that they will have a helper through life. We will have comfort. The Lord is present in our trials and our painful experiences. Trusting Him will come easier when you spend time with Him so He can speak help, hope, and direction to you.

RESPONSE:

_____

_____

_____

_____

_____

_____

_____

_____

_____

_____

_____

_____

_____

_____

_____

_____

_____

_____

_____

_____

_____

_____

JOYLESS, NUMB, AND RIDDLED WITH GUILT

Yikes, that's a tough title. But it's true for anyone who has experienced moral injury. In its simplest definition, it is an injury to the soul. It is an injury to the conscious. Your soul is the part of you consisting of mind, will, and emotions. It is your true nature. With soul injury, it feels to the person affected that they have lost their sense of self, whereas moral injury causes moral confusion due to one's deeply held beliefs. Moral injury is not considered a mental illness, but many have such negative thoughts about themselves that the potential is there for it to develop into mental health conditions. The one thing that is certain is it will debilitate a person. The moral ambiguities eat away fiercely. It seems like the regrets go on for an extensive time, and the individual may feel quite haunted by the occurrence(s).

Sonya Norman, PhD, and Shira Maguen, PhD, wrote an article on moral injury[31] with a very good explanation. The highlights are: In traumatic or unusually stressful circumstances, people may perpetuate, fail to prevent, or witness events that contradict deeply held moral beliefs and expectations. When someone does something that goes against their beliefs, this is often referred to as an act of commission, and when they fail to do something in line with

---

31 Norman, Sonya and Shira Maguen. Moral Injury, April 20, 2020. https://www.ptsd.va.gov/professional/treat/cooccurring/moral_injury.asp.

their beliefs, it is often referred to as an act of omission. In order for moral injury to occur, the individual must feel like a transgression occurred and that they or someone else crossed a line with respect to their moral beliefs. The result is guilt, shame, disgust, anger, and an inability to self-forgive, which can be linked to self-sabotaging behaviors. It can also have an impact on a person's spirituality.

In referring to military personnel or first responders, there is an inner distress or conflict between their moral beliefs and their actions during military service. An example would be killing or harming others accidentally or intentionally. There may have been a person in authority who made a decision that could involve a loss of lives or maimed lives. Those considered first responders could be largely affected by moral injury due to their own moral beliefs and feeling betrayed by those in charge who made decisions in risky scenarios. An example would be an order to leave a burning building when victims are still inside and cannot be reached. In the medical field, decisions have to be made regarding life and death and prioritizing or triaging who gets treated first. What an emotional struggle can occur if not all patients can be saved. How trying it is for a healthcare worker who cannot care for someone due to understaffing, and a decision has to be made on who lives and who dies. Any high-stakes environments and all forms of injustice can cause moral injury.

What trauma can be wrought by a person who trusts another who fails to do the right thing? Or you serve your country, and upon returning home, people respond very negatively to you by name-calling, spitting, or throwing paint at you. Those who returned from Vietnam felt condemned, abandoned, and emotionally very anguished. I hate that. There is a strong possibility that a woman who aborts a pregnancy will have moral agony. There could be soul injury to an elderly person who feels useless and unseen. There are personal identity issues with someone who is struggling after a divorce, death, or lay-off who has soul injuries as they attempt to find themselves. Soul injury can occur after being abandoned or having a sexual orientation not of "the norm."

But the focus here is mostly on moral injury. Syracuse University wrote *The Moral Injury Project*.[32] These are their examples of moral injury:

1. Using deadly force in combat and causing the harm or death of civilians, knowingly but without alternatives, or accidentally.

2. Giving orders in combat that result in the injury or death of a fellow service member.

3. Failing to provide medical aid to an injured civilian or service member.

4. Returning home from deployment and hearing of the executions of cooperating local nationals.

5. Failing to report knowledge of a sexual assault or rape committed against oneself, a fellow service member, or civilians.

6. Following orders that were illegal, immoral, or against the Rules of Engagement (ROE) or Geneva Convention.

7. A change in belief about the necessity or justification for war during or after one's service.

War is not the only thing that can cause damage to the soul. Abuse, rape, and any act of violence can cause it. So, essentially, any exposure to trauma. Many healthcare workers during the

---

32 "What Is Moral Injury." *The Moral Injury Project*, What is Moral Injury. Accessed September 4, 2023. https://moralinjuryproject. edu/about-moral-injury/.syr.

COVID crisis experienced moral injury and burnout. Moral injury does not show up immediately; it can be days, months, or years. It can result in increasing anxiety, depression, insomnia, and post-traumatic stress, and it can bring on suicidal thoughts. There is also spiritual and social suffering. Research recorded that 90 percent of veterans have moral injury, a staggering statistic.

Moral injury can be considered a social, psychological, and even spiritual suffering stemming from one's attempts to manage, control, or cope with one's moral dilemma(s). Have you ever wondered if there was a Bible character with moral injury? Would you consider that one to be King David, as he had ordered the murder of Uriah, and he abused his power to lure Bathsheba to him for sexual reasons? Would you consider the apostle Paul having moral injury as he was involved in a very heavy dose of persecuting Christians before he was blinded on the road to Damascus and changed his horrid ways? Possibly, afterward, his conscience may have been talking to him. Elijah was a mighty prophet who ordered the killing of 450 prophets of Baal. Under the threat of being killed, it caused him to flee, be depressed and suicidal. Did you ever wonder if any of those who stoned Stephen to death regret their involvement in what they did to an innocent man? I wonder if Cain had a moral conflict when he murdered his own brother. In 2 Kings 15:23–25, fifty guards help the king's chief officer, Pekah, murder King Pekahiah of Israel. It would be hard to imagine that all fifty of those men had no emotional trouble after following that order.

I would consider all of the above as having damage to their soul, some more and some to a lesser degree. Maybe you want to ponder their events. But, let me talk about King Saul as having moral injury. He was rejected by God and thus lost fellowship with God, whereas the spirit of the Lord departed from Saul, and a harmful spirit came on him (1 Samuel 16:14). This was also mentioned in three other places. It was torment. His life was one of murderous thoughts, one focused on exalting himself, being fearful, suspicious, angry, and very jealous. He had significant mood swings. He saw war as it is recorded that in a battle with the Philistines, they pressed hard against Saul, and he was badly wounded by the archers. I expect he had combat trauma. He asked his armor-bearer to kill him, but he refused, so Saul took his own life. For forty-two years, he reigned as an ungodly king. But King Saul had lost his mind, lost his grip on his life, and in today's age, we would have had him baker acted for his irrational behavior. He was not Saul the Sane but Saul the unstable, unglued, unsound, and unpredictable. You get it. Saul was a man with a tragic life.

Why does guilt feel so full of anxiety? It is associated with the prefrontal cortex, where logical thinking takes place. It also causes problems with the limbic system. Guilt is a bad feeling due to one's thinking they did something wrong or bad. Anxiety causes the feeling, but guilt is the result.

With moral injury, a person may engage in self-sabotaging behaviors. It all starts with listening to your inner voice telling you that you do not deserve to feel better. That is an erroneous belief. Your inner voice is telling you that you don't deserve love and you are a terrible person or a failure. Get that out of your head and heart immediately. It could manifest as self-medicating, self-injury, or more subtly as procrastination or disorganization. Possibly, you feel overwhelmed, so you just fold like a lawn chair instead of fighting through for your own good.

Moral injury is not post-traumatic stress (PTS), nor is it post-traumatic stress disorder (PTSD). They share symptoms such as guilt, anger, depression, addictive behaviors, and trouble maintaining meaningful relationships. PTSD is mostly treated as a mental or physical disorder with medication and counseling. Trauma of any sort changes you. Trauma is a life issue. With either, hope gets lost, but keep in mind that we are never without hope.

SKILLS TO TRY:

1. Prolonged exposure (PE) is known to be effective, so I recommend you contact a licensed therapist who specializes in it. It is a form of cognitive behavior therapy involving trauma-focused talk where you are taught not to be afraid of the memory. One gradually approaches the memories, feelings, and situations that you have avoided. You face your fears. It helps you have fewer unwanted memories.

2. One can benefit from learning breathing techniques to reduce anxiety.

3. This is a no-brainer. Create your environment so you make the time and space for your well-being. This includes physical well-being, such as your exercise routine, sleep schedule and comfort, healthy meals, and stress management, such as meditation/prayer. Make a list of what you want for your own treatment plan, and then get suggestions from skilled and trusted people who can help you make that happen. For example, if you want to work on loss of trust or intimacy, then divulge that to a skilled individual who can help.

4. Find your purpose. My first book, *Stuff Your Fanny Pack with Coping Skills*, addressed this from pages 287–305. This will help you focus on what matters and prioritize your life. Trauma changed you, but finding purpose helps you be optimistic in spite of those changes that don't feel good, and it creates resiliency so you can be Bo Bounce Back or Snana Snap Back.

5. Have you noticed any self-sabotaging behaviors or emotions? They may be very subtle, such as feeling fearful, unworthy, insecure, or just indecisive. Name what you are feeling and apply a healthy coping skill to it. An unhealthy activity would be to get drunk or high or put down a half bucket of fried chicken and half a chocolate cake. Yes, I know your taste buds will be thrilled, but it will not help you cope. A healthy skill would be to practice deep breathing, go for a run, or talk to a supportive friend or family member. They should not be surprised to hear you say you are self-sabotaging a relationship or are putting your job in jeopardy and will likely have ideas for you. Hopefully, they make you accountable to stop the destructive cycle. You have to check for negative messages you are telling yourself, such as "I don't deserve to have Lovely Lori for my girlfriend," or, "Smartie Pants Smithy should have been hired, not me." You must learn to recognize that you are saying or doing things that are blocking your success and then replace them with helpful messages. When you stop the negative messages, and it will take some time and practice, you should see a positive shift to an improved mood instead of a maladaptive one.

6. Oh, that guilt! But guilt implies you did something wrong. Maybe it was not wrong to follow an order by a superior. It could be misplaced guilt. Maybe you didn't act as you should have or failed by omission. Maybe the guilt was brought on by others. But it is essentially regret as you perceive you caused harm to someone or you went against your morals. You must ask yourself if you did something to feel guilty for or if somebody else is making you feel guilty. Then, ask yourself if there

is anything about the situation you can control. Can amends be made? If so, examine what can be done. If the situation involves a person who has died or a scenario that you cannot return to, then writing down your thoughts can be helpful. While doing this, show yourself some love and kindness. It is called history, so it's behind you. Why would you drag it into your present or future? Let go and let joy in. Swap guilt for grace. That's God's ability to work in and through and for you. It will require that you ask for His help and then accept it.

"As far as the East is from the West, so far has He removed our transgressions from us" (Psalm 103:12, NIV).

How is that for good news? It means an infinite distance. Breathe that revelation in like the best breath you have ever taken.

RESPONSE:

COLLATERAL DAMAGE

When I say collateral damage, I really mean secondary trauma. Collateral damage means any damage incidental to an activity.[33] Secondary trauma is very close to compassion fatigue, vicarious trauma, or secondary traumatic stress with minor differences. Compassion fatigue has to do with being worn out emotionally and physically due to helping another and, from that, not being able to fully take care of oneself and revive oneself. Vicarious trauma is a negative reaction in one's worldview that is changed to the exposure to the trauma content/material. Secondary traumatic stress occurs when the providers experience post-traumatic stress-like symptoms without having been directly exposed to the trauma. For now, secondary trauma means someone is significantly affected by another person's trauma. It is a stress response upon hearing or witnessing the trauma of another. You could say those who fit that category are "indirect victims." I will use the term victim loosely for understanding purposes only.

Secondary trauma is a common stress reaction for those who are first responders, social workers, child welfare workers, and mental health professionals. It can be especially difficult for those who work shifts in fields such as burn units, brain injury units, psychiatric wards, emergency rooms, those who are crime scene

---

33 "Collateral Damage Definition & Meaning." Dictionary.com. Accessed September 3, 2023. https://www.dictionary.com/browse/collateral-damage.

investigators, disaster responders, and those who are police and firefighters. It can also come from being the parent of a child or the child of a parent who has experienced trauma. There are others. Secondary trauma can also be an isolated incident. Those who listen to or witness other people's vivid and explicit injuries or stories are quite susceptible. I often tell people to be sure to take care of themselves as the "caregiving" occupations can cause major fatigue, and their own needs often get put on the back burner. These necessary, vital fields can be most taxing, so again, take care of yourself and individualize what care you need. What helps one person destress is different for another. For example, I find my dog comforting, but for others, a dog could be irritating.

Between 40 and 85 percent of professionals in the helping field develop vicarious trauma, compassion fatigue, or high rates of traumatic symptoms.[34] The stakes are high, so employing coping skills is extremely important, as well as it helps with making attempts to find life balance.

Signs of secondary trauma fall into physical, emotional, and behavioral symptoms. Some that I will highlight are feeling emotionally exhausted, increased depression and anxiety, having a new fear, worrying excessively, insomnia, anger, increased use of drugs and alcohol, difficulty making decisions, increased problems in relationships, feeling helpless and hopeless, feeling guilty and cynical, loss of pleasure, difficulty separating work and home life and even having suicidal ideation.

Matthew 14, Mark 6, and Luke 9 all tell a story that could be considered secondary trauma as an isolated incident. Herod the Tetrarch (ruler of a Roman providence) had dinner guests for his birthday, and during that occasion, his brother's wife, Herodias, whom Herod had seduced, had a daughter that danced so well (likely sensual) that he gave her a promise she could have whatev-

---

34 Mathieu, Francoise, 2012.

er she wanted. Prompted by her mother, who was cruel and wanted revenge, influenced her daughter to ask for John the Baptist's head on a platter. Of all the things she could have asked for. The problem arose when John had previously spoken to Herod, who was not a moral man but actually weak and depraved, about his inappropriate relationship with Herodias. Now, I gave myself a visual of that scene where, indeed, John's head was brought to the girl on a platter. Herod's guests and disciples all would have seen this. It would be an incident that would indelibly stay in one's brain, especially for those who loved John the Baptist.

Kelly Simpson for "Christian Living" wrote about helping the traumatized on June 25, 2021. Her points in this paragraph are a valid lesson for us that Jesus offered trauma stewardship. It is wise caregiving, not ownership. It is the imperfect, messy practice of lamenting with others and helping them walk a difficult road. Jesus' life was one where He neither blocked out human trauma nor became absorbed by it. He drew near and was compassionate. He experienced and understood our grief. He didn't stand aloof, but He entered into a world filled with trauma: "The word became flesh and dwelt among us" (John 1:14, ESV). Jesus cried for his friends (John 11:35), struggled through His own trauma (Luke 22:40–46), and asked friends to stay with Him in His pain (Matthew 26:36–38). Jesus practiced "omnipotent compassion" for the wounded, traumatized sheep without a shepherd (Mark 6:30–34). There was power in His presence and care, not only for physical healing but for psychological and relational healing as well. As the Lord walked the earth, He was not swallowed by grief. He never despaired or lost hope. Sometimes, He retreated when crowds needed Him (Luke 5:15–16) and napped when others were in crisis (Mark 4:38). He was not always available to everyone in need. He retreated to pray and rest in order to re-engage later (Mark 1:35–39).

SKILLS TO TRY:

1. With secondary trauma, you have been indirectly exposed to it by hearing or seeing the disturbing things of other people's trauma. It is a must to take care of yourself. This means making a plan for your self-care. I worked in a jail and heard a lot of negative, distressing reports virtually all day. I read some unsettling police reports so I could accurately house the clients in case they were suicidal or had mental illnesses. My self-care plan was to be on time for work but to leave on time. It was a boundary I set. I needed to shake it off on my way home the best I could and try to get the stories out of my head. Changing work clothes to comfy clothes was a part of shedding work. Getting out in nature for a walk was also helpful.

2. Oddly enough, having a sense of humor was a great coping skill for me to employ in a jail mental health office. Fortunately, my coworkers also had a great sense of humor. So, I am recommending that you find some fun and funny people you connect with and places and things to have a laugh over.

3. Develop the skill of detaching from the other person's traumatic ordeal. You will need to see if you are "too involved" in another person's suffering. You can lose yourself in their painful experience to the point it takes over your own life. First, ask yourself why you may need to detach. Maybe it is because the stories have become problematic for you in some way, such as causing you to lose sleep or triggering something you personally have been traumatized about. To detach means you release your own emotions, not bottle them up, and you

respond, not react. You can still care and show empathy and help, but you let another person know what you can and cannot do.

4. Due to the nature of being in a caring field where you may see and hear the unthinkable on a regular basis, it is important to find things that are positive and rewarding to balance it all out. You will need to individualize what it is for you. Consider your favorite meal or treat, an activity where you release tension, the music you can sing or dance to, a favorite place to visit long distance or a shorter jaunt, a shopping trip, and time with someone who listens well and makes you feel happy to be around. Have a place to go, like a workshop, garden, workout room, or craft room. Have several ideas, but be tenacious about incorporating them. Have more ideas that you can switch out for another week.

5. When things you have seen and heard have been so barbarous, and it compounds for the next day, and so on, then it becomes vital to monitor your own negative thinking so you don't feel helplessly sucked into the world of blood and crud. You have spent your day being compassionate and helpful to a traumatized individual(s), and from that, there could be some residual effects on yourself. Be aware and be proactive.

6. Get creative. This allows you to express yourself and use both sides of your brain: the creative and the logical side. Whatever you are working on, whether painting, chalk art, pottery, cooking, making flies for fishing, whittling, or drawing, it gives you time to quiet your brain. It is getting in touch with the simpler side of life.

7. I can always recommend to get in nature. Nature nur-

tures. I do this daily as my senses are nicely activated, and it helps when I look at its beauty to get the police and client reports out of my head.

8. Set boundaries. You could set the clock by me that I worked hard and steadily, but when it was time to leave, it was "adios." It was how I balanced the pressures of work and could breathe a sigh of relief to change my atmosphere to the peace of home. If your home is not peaceful or quiet due to various reasons of having children and responsibilities or ongoing drama, then a trip to the gym or sitting in your vehicle and taking time to shake it off first may be a necessity. Talk to who is in your home and explain that you need some unwind time, then you can go with children and spouse/partner activities. Maybe there is a hobby you can take a few minutes to incorporate, such as photography or doodling. What boundaries or limits do you need to set? Do you say no when you need to? Are your days off prioritized for yourself and your family? If people pull on you for your time when you are off for a day, then consider setting a limit to your availability, if it's possible. With all this, be considerate of what the household members need.

9. It is a positive thing to express how you have helped others, especially those in helping professions. In my case, it seemed to make me feel that it was all worthwhile and I was helping. That counteracted the negative. It's not bragging—it's good mental health. For those in leadership positions, acknowledgments such as monetary tokens or gift cards cause the tired and stressed to feel like they contributed and it was recognized. If not that course of action, then emails of "atta

boy or girl" or a meeting where one's extra mile effort gets mentioned helps a person feel that they can do it again tomorrow.

10. Try journaling. Writing down what you are emotional about helps you feel like you can control at least some aspects of the hard stuff. It gives you a positive way to express your feelings. This only takes a few minutes. Your journaling may include drawings or stickers. Nobody is too old for stickers. Pick the ones you love. The dollar stores have them cheap, or you can make your own. Be sure you are in a comfortable place to do your journaling. Maybe even name it something like "my unwind place" or "my destress spot." Mine is the porch because I have a colorful visual of my flowers and butterflies.

11. In the above article, the author, Kelly Simpson, reports she practices trauma stewardship by using wisdom and discernment about when to retreat and rest. She adds she won't always carry the burdens of others as she was not designed to. Therefore, she casts her cares on the Lord (1 Peter 5:7), both her own and for others. She reminds her "others" about the power, advocacy, strength, and comfort of the Holy Spirit. She concludes that trauma stewardship honors the survivor, the pain, the story, and one's limitations. It abides in hope and honors God, who never wastes pain. With all that, I implore you to consider your perspective on all of this, what you have learned, and what you need to tweak or apply. Always consult the Lord, who knows all, sees all, and has the perfect plan.

12. If you have experienced trauma, there is the possibility

that you will have a harder time looking at God as loving, forgiving, and present for you. However, many go through a spiritual crisis after a trauma. You can mourn the situation or suffering you were caused. God understands when we question Him, and we need answers. God is magnificent, sees all, knows all, and has all the resources to cause things to work out in the end. It will be what is the best-case scenario for us, with love, mercy, grace, and good favor all over it. If need be, get a trusted spiritual advisor who can help you with your perspective. After all, one's emotions are a bit out of whack from the unsettling life events. Think about a time when your faith was high. Can you recreate some of that to remind yourself that faith works?

13. Get support and seek a professional counselor if necessary. They should be a person who can utilize their active listening skills and offer a helpful perspective as well as give you skills for getting you through the trauma that feels overwhelming. Don't let pride hold you back. We all need help every now and then.

"But let all who take refuge in you be glad; let them ever sing for joy. Spread your protection over them, that those who love your name may rejoice in you" (Psalm 5:11, NIV).

It is David in this psalm praying for protection. He exhorts us to take refuge in God and be glad. How can a person be glad after suffering? Try knowing God loves you even if it is hard to feel it. Try believing that God is aware of everything that concerns you and is working on all of it.

RESPONSE:

_____

_____

_____

_____

_____

_____

_____

_____

_____

_____

_____

_____

_____

_____

_____

_____

_____

_____

_____

_____

_____

_____

_____

THE HAPPIEST CREATURE

Consider once again the title of this book, "Trauma Reversed." That most likely has not fully happened for you, but neither are you done with the work that needs to happen. You will make decisions every day on whether or not to fight through the challenges towards a life that makes you feel happier and more whole in every way—mentally, physically, emotionally, socially, relationally, financially, and spiritually. You hopefully believe more in yourself, and you are certainly wiser.

I want you to feel like a quokka (pronounced "kwaa kuh"). You probably have to look it up. I did, too. It's the happiest creature on earth, according to National Geographic.[35] Okay, I will tell you what this little creature is. It's a small Wallaby about the size of a cat. Their little faces are full of cuteness overload with a look like they are perpetually smiling. That's because of the shape of their mouth. They have a friendly and playful disposition as well. They live in Australia and are also called joeys. They are herbivores. If times are lean, they store fat in their tails. Quokkas have an abdominal pouch to carry their babies. While threatened, adult quokkas are known to throw their babies out of their pouches to

---

35 Reese, April. "'World's Happiest Animal' Bouncing Back, Thanks to Golf." Science, July 13, 2017.   https://www.nationalgeographic.com/science/article/quokka-selfies-australia-golf-tourism-animals.

serve as a distraction and allow them ample time to get away from the threat.[36] The cuteness has now left.

Their nature is to be gentle and sweet. Touching them is a serious no-no with a potential fine. Quokkas get around by hopping, bounding, and moving forward with their hands. They share space, food, and shelter with each other, unlike their boxing relatives, the kangaroos.

Some places where the quokkas inhabit have no predators, but in other places, they have dingoes, birds of prey, and snakes. Cats and dogs were later introduced. But if confronted, a male quokka will let out a shriek in hopes of scaring off their predators.

So, dear reader, what does a quokka have to do with you? It's about the happiness! Happiness is defined as an enduring state of mind consisting not only of feelings of joy, contentment, and other positive emotions but also of a sense that one's life is meaningful and valued.[37] So, with those emotions, can you even remember when was the last time you had a "quokka" type smile on your face and felt those emotions of joy, contentment, and that your life had meaning and you were valued? It is hard to look cute when downcast. I expect you have not had a good mood long enough to hop and bound around.

What about predators? Did you have any? Do you have any now? By that, I mean a predator is someone who tries to exploit or oppress others. The human one tries to exert power over another. They seek to control and dominate. They mean to injure. In the animal world, a predator may hunt or lay in wait for their prey, or they can camouflage themselves to grab their intended victim. A human predator will prey on a person they observe as being weak or vulnerable. That could include someone in need of attention or

---

36 Best Life Editors, July 11, 2019.
37 Lyubomirsky, 2001.

love, a child, an intoxicated person, a person with infirmities, aged, or a person vulnerable due to their location, such as being in a dark area. The human predator will attempt to be charming, use intimidation, coercion, deception, and isolation, and trap you to get you to do anything they want. They are tricky liars, and it's about all that they can gain and who they can manipulate. They work to get the person's trust, as in a sexual predator. In those cases, they will try and create a special bond with a child in particular, then move to very inappropriate responses. They are out there.

This was not at all meant to be triggering. It was to give insight and then skills. It was to open your eyes to what could be out there and for you to exercise great awareness. That is not to be paranoid but to be apprised of the signs. If you have been the victim of a predator and that is the cause of your trauma, once again, there is hope. Yes, hope and treatment. Trauma is history, and life with happiness is ahead of you with some workable plans, goals, wisdom, tangible help, and people who care and can be trusted. Remember your past is back there, make your future.

Suffering is universal. Victimhood is optional. At some point, we will suffer some kind of affliction, calamity, or abuse caused by circumstances or people or institutions over which we have little or no control. This is life. And that is victimization. It comes from the outside. It's the neighborhood bully, the boss who enrages, the spouse who hits, the lover who cheats, the discriminatory law, or the accident that lands you in the hospital. In contrast, victimhood comes from the inside. No one can make you a victim but you. We become victims not because of what happens to us but when we choose to hold onto our victimization. We develop a victim's mind: a way of thinking and being that is rigid, blaming, pessimistic, stuck in the past, unforgiving, punitive, and without healthy limits or boundaries.[38]

---

38 Edith Eger, *The Choice: Embrace the Possible.* 2017.

Cambridge Dictionary defines victimhood as the condition of having been hurt, damaged, or made to suffer, especially when you want people to feel sorry for you because of this or use it as an excuse for something.[39] In other words, victimhood or victim mentality is a person who considers themselves a victim of the negative actions of others. A person who has had a lot of trauma has no control and feels helpless or trapped. This is mentioned so you may relate that it could be you, and once you recognize yourself, you decide you will not stay in that unhealthy state of thinking.

SKILLS TO TRY:

1. Allow yourself to feel the pain. Know it will not last forever. It will ease up. Remember, it's a normal reaction to an abnormal event. Emotions do need to be expressed. For some, it is hard to do as they might not know exactly how they feel or they have a notion that it is weak to do so. This is erroneous as it is quite empowering. In sharing, start with something you can feel at least a little comfortable with.

2. Look at the last paragraph. Where are you with your thinking? Are you in a mindset of victimhood? Think this through carefully. If so, change your thinking from what you don't have to what you do have. You must stop thinking you drew the short straw and life handed you a bucket of unfairness. Instead, map out how you will be the master of your destiny. Find meaning. Really, what does that look like for you? The opposite of victimhood is empowerment and resiliency. Take responsibility.

3. Don't blame others. Blaming will hurt relationships. It

39 *"Victimhood." Cambridge Dictionary. Accessed September 3, 2023. https:// dictionary.cambridge.org/dictionary/english/victimhood.*

can also lead one to hold anger, resentment, and even hatred. By saying that someone else did such and such, you don't take responsibility for your own actions. Blaming others is a form of putting them down. So, no blaming and shaming. Learn and allow others to learn from their errors.

4. If you feel like you do not have control over anything or much in your life, then make goals for yourself—little ones, medium ones, and long-range goals. Give positive feedback to yourself when they are achieved. For example, getting registered for school is a small goal, finishing a semester is a medium-sized goal, and graduation is a big, long-range goal. Look at your progress, not what seems to be disappointments. Because what you think of as a failure may be a learning experience, or maybe you can think of it as such, to feel less beat up emotionally.

5. Make daily decisions that will help you feel like normalcy is possible and help you feel like you have some control. Don't make major decisions right away, as you may feel overwhelmed and stressed, and negative hormones may be high.

6. Now, about that quokka's grin and being happy. What are the practical things you can do to get your stress under control? Treat yourself well. That means being your own bestie. If you need a treat, get one, and if you need a timeout or break, then take it. If you need positive people, interactions, and activities, make those adjustments. Walk the dog for an exercise benefit and sit outdoors in the sunlight. Fit in hammock time with a good book and laughter with a friend. Practice self-

care to the ultimate. Read, pray, and sing. Don't talk down to yourself. Take from the movie *Top Gun* those moments where you hear "Take My Breathe Away." Create what you need.

In my quest for quokka moments, I start my day at about 5:30 a.m. to begin the day by giving God His due praise and praying. Then it's hot tea and talk time with my husband. My little rescue dog Annie will not be forgotten, so she gets her petting time and walk time. I will check on my garden and take it all in with my senses. Then to the computer. But friends and family may have things they need from me, or I get grandchildren's time on weekends. I will do my best to honor that. The afternoon and then evening are reading time, another walk, a good meal, and my favorite show to wind down from the day. For some reason, the simplicity of my day is my quokka moment. Okay, make your list to add those moments that bring on a smile and a move in the direction of being happier. Then notice the grin when it comes and do more of what caused that.

7. While you work on changes that help you kick the thinking of victimhood, try being resilient, tough, and full of fortitude. Fortitude means strong and primarily strength of mind. It sounds so good. Be full of the Spirit of God. That means allowing the Holy Spirit to be part of every bit of your life. It's quite wonderful that it brings joy and peace. Guidance comes along like a good cousin. Current troubles and a negative history seem to go more on the back burner and less in your face. Or you at least learn that they can be like water off a duck's back.

8. What were the things you did in the past that helped you cope when things were difficult? Employ those resources. What gave you hope? Add those in generously.

9. Simplify life and its tasks for now. Can you illicit others to help with meals, school pickups, and shopping? It's temporary. It's about nurturing you. Right after a trauma, you need mind and body self-care. This includes the right foods, the best sleep you can get, and exercise. Don't forget time to be alone as well. It will help your brain to reset.

10. There are several words I would like for you to hold onto like a teddy bear. The first one is "to begin." Or try to undertake, commence, launch, or arise. Maybe it's an expression such as bring to pass, embark on, get going, set up, or set in motion. But do something to not stay stuck or immobile. I personally like the word "embark" as it suggests I am going somewhere, and it means action. Move out of misery and into a new beginning, tough or not tough scenario; you are moving.

11. There is a website for the Office for Victims of Crime in the Department of Justice.[40] It has a two-page list of services, including ways to call, text, or email. You can also watch on YouTube under "Office of Victims of Crime."

"Defend the cause of the weak and fatherless; maintain the rights of the poor and oppressed. Rescue the weak and needy; deliver them from the hand of the wicked" (Psalm 82:3–4, NIV).

It seems like we can turn it into a prayer to help the weak, needy, fatherless, poor, and oppressed. Defend and rescue those

---

40 https://ovc.ojp.gov/helplines

afflicted. I recall a wise pastor saying that what we need for ourselves, pray that for others. At the very least, do something!

RESPONSE:

MARY, MARY QUITE CONTRARY

That title comes from an English nursery rhyme. It goes like this:

Mary, Mary quite contrary,

How does your garden grow?

With silver bells and cockle shells,

And pretty maids all in a row.

But, if you are a trauma survivor, your Mary, Mary rhyme might go like this:

Mary, Mary, quite unhappy,

How does your garden grow?

With doubt, and fear and feeling no cheer,

And heartache lined all in a row.

This is where I am trying to take you. Latch onto the possibilities.

Mary, Mary, quite content,

How does your garden grow?

With no sorrow or fear and nary a tear,

And emotional strength and hope all in a row.

It's not about how your garden grows but how you grow. It's called post-traumatic growth. You might not be able to picture it yet, but survivors of trauma can do more than just survive. They can thrive. I even like the word flourish. Wikipedia reports that post-traumatic growth in psychology is a concept describing positive psychological change experienced as a result of struggling with highly challenging, highly stressful life circumstances.[41]

Dr. Marianne Trent reports examples of growth include personal strength, appreciation for life, new possibilities in life, spiritual change, and relationships with others. Dr. Trent adds some examples can be writing books, finding God, and starting charities. Environmental psychologist Lee Chambers reports that post-traumatic growth can show up by uncovering latent talent and ability, finding the confidence to face new challenges, and discovering a feeling of strength.

My story of growth after several years of a "boatload of highly stressful events" was drawing even closer to God and seeing how He came through for me and mine. I also recognized my support was very intact and there for me. A desire to help others welled up in me, so I enrolled in mental health counseling for my master's degree. And you are reading my latent talent to write books. Creativity was drawn out. I discovered that where I felt like I was underestimated and "not quite enough" was growing into a very

---

41 *"Post-Traumatic Growth." Wikipedia, August 13, 2023. https://en.wikipedia. org/wiki/Post-traumatic_growth.*

strong and resilient woman. I desire to be an instrument for noble purposes, made holy, useful to the master, and prepared to do any good work (2 Timothy 2:21b). I will give the Lord credit as I was very much in need of divine intervention. My church, family, and friends were and still are those who encouraged me with "You're gonna make it."

Lee Chambers continues that post-traumatic growth tends to generate a level of mindfulness and gratitude for life and a focus on those relationships that should be prioritized, usually, those that the individual feels were there for them in difficult times. Other often-reported outcomes are a desire to help others and give back, appreciation for life, more self-awareness, and more compassion.

Post-traumatic growth was developed by psychologists Richard Tedeschi, PhD, and Lawrence Calhoun, PhD, in the mid-1990s. The premise is that people who have experienced and endured psychological struggle/trauma often see positive growth afterward. It is slightly different from resilience. Resiliency is an ability to bounce back after difficulty, whereas post-traumatic growth is about what happens to a person after a traumatic event where their core beliefs are challenged, and they find a sense of personal growth. If you are already resilient, then you may not experience post-traumatic growth as your core beliefs are not altered, so you don't have to have a new belief system. Some people will have great distress as they try to figure out the "whys" of the situation and what to do with their altered world now.

Why do some people grow from trauma, and others feel like they want to be buried? Dr. Trent and Lee Chambers explain that a strong support system plays a vital role. Personality traits also play a role, such as extraversion (which is the tendency to experience positive emotions, as well as being sociable, lively, active, and open). Optimism and being future-focused help one to see the upside and utilize it. Integrating the experience into one's life helps an individual not stay in a traumatized state and thus feel stuck.

I am going to give you an unusual comparison but a fascinating one. Let's consider how a ship gets through the Panama Locks. The Atlantic and Pacific Oceans meet at the southern tip of South America, called Cape Horn. The Pacific Ocean stands higher (40 centimeters or 43.7 yards) than the Atlantic Ocean. Traveling around Cape Horn is a treacherous journey by ship. It seems to be due to intense low-pressure systems whirling the sea into humongous waves, creating great violent wind gusts that occur frequently and without notice. Mariners have reported they have seen waves reach 200 feet. Cape Horn has been known to be "the end of the world" or "the largest underwater cemetery." It has been estimated that at least 800 ships were shipwrecked, causing over 10,000 deaths of their seamen over the last few centuries. Obviously, that explains the need for a safer route.

So, you might be wondering how that has anything to do with post-traumatic growth. Pretend that you are a ship coming in from the Atlantic side and need to go through the locks. First of all, you need to do some pre-arrival preparation. You will need the right documents and an inspector to board and investigate as to whether or not you are in good condition. If that is all in order, you can proceed into the locks, which lift you up by water about 85 feet (until sea level), and then you cross about 21 miles on a man-made lake called Gatun Lake. Then, you are lowered by the locks. This takes about eight hours.

You don't need to go through the merciless Cape Horn (let's call it "The Devil's Destructive Deep Dropoff"), as God has provided you with the best route ever. It's the route with His Son Jesus. We can call that your Life Lake or your own Panama Canal, and it is your miracle (Panama locks are called an engineering miracle). Your preparation work is to have and keep things in order by which you hopefully have invited the Lord into your life to accomplish that feat. Your inspector, the Holy Spirit, needs to be on board. He's your guide to help you through the uneven places (the different and difficult sea levels of your trauma). He will lift you up, give you a smooth ride, and then, when necessary and appropriate, lower you back to deal with life. The water lifts, floats, and lowers. Water in the Bible symbolizes life. Water also serves to generate power for the Canal, and spiritually, for us, we need Holy Spirit power. The way the holes were designed in the Canal is to control turbulence. Systems were put in place in history to prevent damage and the ship breaking through a guard gate. We need turbulence control! We don't need to be damaged or to damage others, and we need to not break free from where we can learn to withstand, be resilient, and grow.

The following five skills to try come from Positran (positive psychology):

1. Try positive reminiscing. This involves changing a negative habit to a positive one. The example given is that if you need to involve exercise in your life, then bring to mind all successful experiences from the past of exercising.

2. Savoring. This means being fully immersed in, attending to, and appreciating the current experience. Engage with what you are doing, such as enjoying your food, for example, or focusing on what you find most enjoyable. Suggestions to savoring are to share with others the experience or how you enjoyed it, take a mental picture of the event and reminisce about it later, give yourself congratulations, focus on certain elements of the experience and block others out, absorb yourself in the experience, don't think, just sense.

3. Increase hope. Believe in a beneficial outcome by visualizing your best possible self over a period of time.

4. Use your strengths. Use your strengths to harness change. Positive relationships often underlie a successful change.

5. Respond to good news in an active-constructive way. For example, if your partner was able to quit smoking, then you should pay attention to the person, listen, ask questions, and be interested and enthusiastic. Celebrate.

SKILLS FROM ME TO ADD ARE:

1. Are there people you need to deepen the relationship with because they are, for you, positive and helpful? On the flip side, are there people who you need to eliminate in your life because they put you down, use you, abuse you, isolate you, threaten you, or intimidate you? Some relationships just need to go as while in them you felt fear being around them or even unhealthy guilt. Let go of any relationships where the person does not want to grow. Really, how will you personally grow hanging with Stella Stagnant? What benefit is there being with Larry Lowlife? If there has been trauma and it is history now, but you want to move on/up (like the locks lift) and grow into what makes you happy, then also consider who is in your space. I literally mean physical space and head space.

2. Look for the silver lining, even if it is not evident yet. You may have had a tremendous loss, but the grief can co-exist with the hope that things will get better. An example is my son was laid off from his restaurant job due to COVID. He was the sole support for a family

of four and certainly would not have been able to take care of all the responsibilities on an unemployment check. His silver lining was to make use of the off time and go back to school for his engineering degree. His goal was to graduate and get employed again. His resource was the VA.

3. Practice grounding. That is a self-soothing skill when things are starting to spiral out of control, as in too much stress, anxiety is welling up, you feel overwhelmed, or unwanted memory is dogging you. Grounding will keep you in the present. One technique is to find an object that you can describe in detail. Or try singing or taking a belly breath where you have to focus on the notes or the breaths. Pretend you are taking that anxiety and winding it up like a baseball you are about to throw and then throw it into your imaginary outfield. My grounding technique to get me away from any troubling moods is to get in nature and listen to the sounds of it. Savoring chocolate activates my sense of smell, and so does a cup of tea. I can leave my negative emotions behind when I pet my dog. I can also recite Scripture.

4. Check your thinking. That anger, anxiety, frustration, depression, and disenchantment are not helping you get in the right frame of thinking. Watch your focus. Are you focusing on loss, failure, and insecurity? Get busy. What resources are out there for you? What tangible things can you do? This does not mean your head is in the sand, as the challenges do exist, but you will need to look for ways to move ahead. Past trauma of horror can evolve into a better future. It takes time, but yes, it's possible. It takes work, so be willing to put it in.

5. Share your story and help others. You lived. Share your strengths. Inspire others. Share how to not just get through by the skin of your teeth but to thrive. Pay forward. Share how to pick up your broken pieces and make pottery from them. It will be cracked, but a reminder, like a scar, that you did more than survive; you flourished. By the way, whenever I see a scar, it reminds me that someone went through something, and I feel compassion. I also feel like that scar can be a guide to help others.

6. Find courage. Rebuild a better version of you. It is not necessarily the actual trauma that is causing you great emotional pain but how you interpret it. It has altered your life, but you must decide how to re-alter it back to have happiness and peace again. Look past the pain and anguish. Fill in the blank: Today, I will do this _____ to work towards restoring peace and joy. Tomorrow— do that again and the next day again. Do it for a week. See if some positivity rises up.

7. Time is important. There are no magic steps to return you to feeling normal. Time can just take the edge off to allow our minds and body to get better. Be patient with yourself, but cooperate with an intentional plan of healing. Be specific with a plan. I will certainly not minimize the pain you were caused, but as a counselor, I must direct you to the steps of restoration. The greatest restorer is the Lord. He does not waste anything that happens to us. He has the bigger picture planned out. It will be for your benefit and for the benefit of others. He has the greatest qualifications to heal our past and has His hand on our future. He knows how to heal the terrible memories. He knows what He is doing. Trusting

Him would be a brilliant idea.

"So then, just as you received Christ Jesus as Lord, continue to live in Him, rooted and built up in Him, strengthened in the faith as you were taught, and overflowing with thankfulness" (Colossians 2:6–7, NIV).

One can receive Christ and then grow in the faith and the awareness of Him as our lifeline in all things about life. Thankfulness is a no-brainer, and we should make this an always thing. It will surely change that mentality that life is full of trouble to one where you believe God is at work and can deliver you from it.

RESPONSE:

_____

_____

_____

_____

_____

_____

_____

_____

_____

_____

_____

_____

_____

_____

_____

_____

_____

_____

_____

_____

IT IS TIME
FOR A NEW YOU

Pretend you have lived in Trouble Town, then moved to Tribulation Town, and even had a few months at Tumultuous Town. I want you to begin again in a wonderful place called Newu (New you) Town. It is in any county or state you want to be, as you are empowered to decide that. Are you wondering what's there for you? There are new people to meet called Buddies and Blessings; work if you want or need it called Joy Job; a park to walk in called Peace Park. Up for sale at a very good price is a house on Relief Road. I can almost picture you with a box and starting to pack. Okay, it is pie in the sky, or is it? It's up to you.

So, you say you are ready for a new beginning. You desire stress and mess, pain and shame, woes and worries to be history. It's not that life won't have some of that because it is life, but to be equipped to manage it is everything. As you exit your current place of residence, consider if you need to figuratively burn the bridge behind you so the negativity does not cross over to Newu Town.

Here are some encouraging thoughts:

> *"Naysayers have little power over us unless we give it to them."*
>
> **Arianna Huffington**

"Many of life's failures are people who did not realize how close they were to success when they gave up."

Thomas Edison

"Sometimes it takes an unbearable breakdown to have an undeniable breakthrough."

Fearless Soul

"Life becomes easier when you learn to accept an apology you never got."

Robert Brandt

"That's all you can do in this world, no matter how strong the current beats against you, or how heavy your burden, or how tragic your love story. You keep going."

Robyn Schneider

"Keeping baggage from the past will leave no room for happiness in the future."

Wayne l Misner

"Sometimes it takes a heartbreak to shake us awake and help us see we are worth so much more than we're settling for."

Mandy Hale

"Whatever you do, never run back to what broke you."

Frank Ocean

An interesting story of moving to Newu Town is the story of Arnold Schwarzenegger. He was born in Austria. His family was considered poor. His father, Gustav, was a police chief, postal inspector and part of the Nazi party. Arnold reports he considered his father abusive when he would come home drunk once or twice a week.[42]

Arnold moved to the US at age twenty-one to follow his dream of bodybuilding. He moved with not knowing much English. However, he surrounded himself with people who helped him achieve his dreams in bodybuilding and then making Hollywood movies. He had support from gym coaches/trainers, an artist, people who trained him to win competitions, and Hollywood players, to name a few. Arnold took English classes in preparation for success. He also had the support of those who elected him governor of California. Bravo to Arnold—talk about an immigrant who has made a big difference.

So, you may think that is a compelling true story, but connect some dots here. Arnold wanted to escape the abuse he felt like he was experiencing at home, have a better life, and achieve the goals he set. He took the time to take the steps to achieve those goals, even if it took years. He connected with people who could help him be a success. He was very disciplined, determined, strategic, and focused, and he did not let other things get in his way. You probably know his famous quote, "I'll be back." That line Hollywood style was in reference to violence, but you can use it to mean what stops you, you find a way to go around it, over it, or under it. Personally, I like "Hasta la vista, baby," which means "bye." That's bye to what has held you back—people, places, and things. Arnold moved almost six thousand miles. He left what in his heart and mind was an abusive childhood. He stayed in contact with his mother as she was positive. He helped his deceased brother's

---

42 The U.S. Sun

child, as again, that seemed like the right thing to do. I call it paying forward and great benevolence.

The Bible has some stories about people who had to start over. Moses was a murderer who became a fugitive and traveled far away to begin again. David went from shepherd boy to man hiding as he had to run from King Saul, who had murderous thoughts towards him. Esther was an orphan and ended up being displaced from her home due to an edict from the king to come and live in the king's palace. Joseph left a home in which he was loved by his father to end up being thrown in a cistern by his brothers, then to an Egyptian jail for years, essentially forgotten. Elijah had to run from the death threats of Jezebel, where he spent forty days and nights in the wilderness. The disciple John was exiled to the island of Patmos. The apostle Paul spent three years in Arabia and three occasions in jail, which totaled approximately five and a half years in custody. God told Abraham, who was very much a senior, to leave his country, his people, and his father's household to go to a land that God would show him. Jacob moved his whole family from Canaan to Egypt. He also did that at a very old age. Noah took his family and left his home and dry land to live on a boat for forty days and then rebuild on land that you would suppose was soggy. There are more, but all of these had challenges to restart; whether it was forced on them to have to begin again or their choice, they did it under the watchful sovereign eye of God.

My personal story is my mother decided "enough of the cold" and moved us two thousand miles from Canada to Florida. It took some serious planning as visas had to be applied for, and the process took a long time. There were three kids and pets to pack up. There were finances to get in order and a house to sell. Emotionally, I knew it was the right decision as the cold was negatively affecting my mother's arthritis. As a teenager, there was a new school to start and friends I had to leave. I wondered if I would ever see them again and how hard it would be to make new friends and adjust to a new school. The move delayed my getting my driver's license, and I never got to go to prom. I never saw those friends again, either.

Our move was outside of our comfort zone, but it was well-planned and intentional. My old home, school, and neighborhood were familiar. A move to a new place would create uncertainty, and I am sure my mother had some worries. There are the unpredictable parts of life. My mom's mother and sister had already died. She missed her father. I had to adjust to a new school system and certainly a weather change. I still wonder if my mom had regrets, but she did what she felt like she needed to do and wanted to do.

So, the point is to not succumb to fear. The comfort zone had a known routine that was well-comfortable and without trouble. It was safe and easy, and we felt in control. Change requires you to change your thinking that whatever needs to be done, you can learn and grow from it. People adapt and learn resilience and develop ways to cope. People do seem to eventually find purpose in their changes.

If you have survived a trauma, then you may not even have a comfort zone. Maybe your house had or has a lot of happenings that make your stress and anxiety high. Maybe even today, as a survivor, you still don't feel safe. If you have that life experience, just start at square one with creating a comfort zone or safe place. This would be creating comforting experiences with how you decorate, dress, eat, and exercise. Maybe start with something simplistic, like a bedspread you love and music that is soothing. Earplugs could be beneficial to decrease the noise from any fighting in the home. Find if there are places like the open park, beach, friend's home, or church where you can feel in control. Be kind to yourself as your brain has been rewired and could be staying in alert mode with all the bells and whistles going off to alert you to danger, even if there isn't danger. But it has been your norm. Much of your life could have been interpreting change as too much of a risk to take or too dangerous. Don't give up on yourself. It's one step at a time, and that step is whatever pace you can do.

Here are some skills for starting over: leaving behind the negative, whether it is abuse, a negative home life, toxic relationships, or personal reasons—it's about you who have tired of feeling impoverished—body, soul, and spirit.

SKILLS FOR STARTING OVER:

1. Consult the Lord always. If you have trouble hearing His direction, then seek a wise spiritual advisor. If you don't have to flee in an emergency, then you have that extra essential time for prayer to gain wisdom and make a solid plan. Jacob longed to see his son Joseph, but he stopped in Beersheba to seek the Lord. I would expect he was emotional as he thought his son was dead and now hears the great news not only is he alive but one of the rulers over Egypt. Talk about life turning around for the good.

2. Consider if you need a safety plan. If so, your new address should be a secret, and use a post office box if needed. Maybe you should get a burner phone. Collect valuables and paperwork that are important. Always make sure kids and pets are safe. Consult an attorney if needed. See a doctor if needed. Have a list of safe people you can ask for help. Have a list of resources to contact if you are in a crisis. I will not make a full list here because I want you to be under the guidance of trustworthy people. It is highly stressful, and I don't

want you to go it alone.

3.   To begin again, if not in a crisis, then plan and make goals. You can give them a name. How about "My PGs" (my personal goals)? Examine your values so none are ignored. Anxiety seems to be part of the unknown. You may have a host of emotions, such as confusion but hopeful or scared but happy. Change is inevitable, and emotions that fluctuate are part of that package. That includes being vulnerable. It's your life, which there is but one to live, and it's your journey to wellness. It's also yours to choose in your way and in your time.

4.   Don't leave behind your bag of courage. Courage is action in spite of fear. Change can be fun but quite challenging. Be self-aware. Get comfortable with being uncomfortable for now. Things usually fall into place, given the time and effort. If you know your values and principles, it's a start for making decisions. You will need to be flexible and take the initiative for change to occur.

5.   Listen to any fears, but don't let them control you. Fear and courage are opposites. If it does not work out as you thought, then don't be afraid of failure. It means you try again or go a different way. If you find the need to be a perfectionist, you will need to let that go. People make mistakes when making decisions, and the burden of doing that in a perfect way will only bog you down.

6.   What is your motivation to move forward? Being unhappy could be one reason. Being used, abused, accused, and refused could be reasons. What about un-

loved and shoved? The character named Steve Urkel on Family Matters, a television show from the 1990s, had a catchphrase: "I've fallen and I can't get up." That sounds like a change is needed. Steve played the role of a son whose parents did not seem to want him. Although he had quite a few incidences of misfortune happen to him and those around him, he got in touch with his strength, and that was his intelligence. It is different for each person.

7. My pep talk is this: You've made it this far; don't quit. The negatives have way taken over any positives, and you may have doubts. That makes you normal. You have survived thus far, and you can continue to survive the changes and recovery. Keep motivated, as the better days will come. You have felt like you have been in a tunnel, and the lights of the train are headed for you, and it does not seem like you can get out. But, with some hope, it's a searchlight, not the lights from a train coming towards you, showing you the way out and forward. Remember your strengths. See your life as full of opportunities, not problems. Develop faith. By doing so, that's a sure thing, and you can't go wrong.

"Forget the former things, do not dwell on the past. See I am doing a new thing!" (Isaiah 43:18–19a, NIV).

God is always there to help a person begin again. Isaiah was telling the people that after their captivity, He would do a new thing. He has a ways and means committee on it for them and for you and your way out to your new thing. That sounds like very good news, especially since the old life was bad news. God wanted the people to stop looking back and look for what was ahead. That has hope all over it. Keep hope. God is the kind of God that wants to do more for you.

RESPONSE:

_____

_____

_____

_____

_____

_____

_____

_____

_____

_____

_____

_____

_____

_____

_____

_____

_____

_____

_____

_____

_____

_____

_____

IT'S THE BEGINNING

We are near the end of the book, but I am calling it the beginning for you. Beginning means the point where something starts. You initiated something as you read through this book about reversing your trauma, and now you continue to emerge as a new you with an improved outlook. Yes, there are still places where life is hard, and yes, there may be evidence by the looks of your bank account for now or even a scar that will be there forever. A scar may represent you survived, or it could mean you learned to cope and be more resilient. What does it mean to you? Make this a positive declaration. The scar means that the body's tissue was injured. God made the body so that when that happens, collagen (a protein) gets released to build the injured tissue to strengthen, support, and heal it. It helps fibroblasts to form in your middle skin layer so new skin cells grow. Make that connection that new skin grows just like you can grow from the negative, maybe even horrific happenings. Be all about the "yes, I can" of it.

Here is an inspirational true story. It was originally from the San Francisco Chronicle on December 14th, 2005.

A massive female humpback whale had become entangled in a spider web of crab traps and lines. She was weighed down by hundreds of pounds of traps, which caused her to struggle to stay afloat. She also had hundreds of yards of line wrapped around her body, her tail, her torso, and a line tugging in her mouth.

A fisherman spotted her just off the coast of San Francisco, California, and he radioed for help. Within a few hours, the rescue team arrived and determined that she was so badly off the only way to save her was to dive in and untangle her. That was a very dangerous proposition, as one slap of the tail could kill a prospective rescuer. They worked for hours with curved knives and eventually freed her.

James Moskito was one of the divers who reported there were about twenty crab-pot ropes, which are 240 feet long and weigh every 60 feet, wrapped around her. The rope was wrapped at least four times around her tail. At least twelve crab traps, weighing about 90 pounds each, hung off the whale, the divers said. The combined weight was pulling the whale downward, forcing it to struggle mightily.

When she was free, the divers say she swam in what seemed like joyous circles. She then came back to each and every diver, one at a time, nudged them, and pushed gently, seemingly thanking them. Nature can be so amazing. Some said it was the most thrilling and incredibly beautiful experience of their lives. The man who cut the rope out of her mouth says her eye was following him the whole time, and he will never be the same from that experience.

This is my little note for you: May you and all those you love be so fortunate as to be surrounded by people who will help you get untangled from the things that are binding you, and may you always know the joy of giving and receiving gratitude.

What about you? You have probably felt heavily weighed down and definitely entangled with much of what life threw at you. The ropes and weights are like oppression, which is defined by the Oxford Dictionary as prolonged, cruel, or unjust treatment or control.[43] It also means mental pressure or distress. Yup, that was life. It was unkind to the max. The whale's benevolent fisherman could have left her, but he got help for her. As I often say, support is everything. I cannot count how many times I have been rescued in a multitude of ways. People paid my bills, paid off my air conditioner loan, put gas in my car, bought me groceries, got my car repaired, had windows installed, babysat, and purchased my children's back-to-school clothes. That is a sampling of things I am grateful for. All of that was needed as I was "entangled and weighed down" badly. However, I will never discount how my "knife," like the one used by the divers to free the whale, was prayer. God came through by using people. All of that was many years ago, but I remain very thankful for it all to this day.

This story reminds me also that we need to leave this book with expressions of gratitude. If you are reading this, then you made it. We are not where we used to be, and we are not where we will yet be. In Luke chapter 10, there is the story of the Good Samaritan. In verse 30 (NIV), it records that "A man was going down from Jerusalem to Jericho, when he was attacked by robbers. They stripped him of his clothes, beat him, and went away leaving him half dead." A priest and a Levite see him but pass him by. But a Samaritan sees him and takes pity on him. He goes the extra mile and bandages his wounds, puts him on his donkey, brings him to an inn, and pays for the expenses with the promise to handle any additional expenses that might occur.

Two men ignored the helpless, wounded stranger. The Good Samaritan represents Christ. We need a savior. We have been broken-hearted and half-dead emotionally, physically, or spiritually.

---

43 "Oppression." oppression noun—Definition, pictures, pronunciation and usage notes | Oxford Advanced Learner's Dictionary at OxfordLearnersDictionaries.com. Accessed September 3, 2023. https://www.oxfordlearnersdictionaries.com/definition/english/oppression.

Remember the song called "Ain't No Mountain High Enough"?[44] Some lyrics are: "If you need me, call me, no matter where you are, no matter how far." That is the character of the Lord, and He is always there for us, promise. It is also the practical side where a Samaritan can be there for us, and we can be a good Samaritan for someone else. It's about love, kindness, compassion, mercy, generosity, and dignity. You have to let others be there. The people who helped me along my road were a mix of males and females, those with finances and those with little, and those young and those who were older. Some were even strangers with a giving spirit who were passing onto us an outpouring of Christ's love when my family needed it desperately due to adverse circumstances.

SKILLS TO TRY:

1. Examine where your weights are and what ropes are tying you up. Are your ropes oppression, poverty, abuse, lack of love, medical or emotional problems? Of course, we will never know what the whale was thinking, but I expect she knew she was in trouble and could perish. She could not save herself. I also wondered how long she had been struggling. As a human, there would be panic. When you are "under" your circumstance, you do feel like you are sinking. Where do you feel like you can sink?

2. As you look at your weights, examine if any weights and ropes are because you are beating yourself up. Why add bruises? We all have shortcomings and weaknesses and make mistakes too numerous to count. That beating yourself up is your thinking where you just focus on all your errors. Stop it and stop it now! Gees, how is that working for you? My first book, *Stuff Your Fanny Pack*

---

44 Gaye, Marvin, and Tammi Terrell. "Ain't No Mountain High Enough." In *United*, album, Tamla Records, 1967.

with Coping Skills, addresses this. But for now, get out of your head where you play it over and over again like a broken record where you messed up.

3. Make a list of where you are sinking, then add a plan to be able to get help; get free. Remember, in the water, it's one stroke at a time. On the ground, it's one step at a time.

4. My curved knife is prayer. It cuts me free from what binds me. How is your spiritual condition? I will not preach to you but only want to remind you that people are made of body, soul, and spirit, and the spirit often gets ignored. When we are down and out, tied up and sinking, it is not a good time to let pride take over. That will sink you. It's always a good time to go to the Lord in prayer and let Him cut away what has restricted you and held you hostage. The whale was held hostage. A whale breathes through the blowhole, their nostril, on the top of their head. It will need to surface in order to breathe. We need to breathe freedom as well.

5. If you have scars, try to have a positive perspective about them. Your body did what it was made to do: heal. It may take time to adjust to whatever was behind the scar. It takes strength to survive. It is not about what you look like, even though you may not have come to terms with it yet. Feel free to embrace that the scars just may be beautiful and have a grand story behind them. My hope is for you to one day be able to say, "Yes, I survived a heart attack, a horrific car accident, a fire, or abuse."

6. Never forget gratitude. When down and out, expressing gratefulness has mental and physical benefits all over

it. Depression, anxiety, worry, fear, stress, and even chronic pain all seem to decrease when we keep an attitude of gratitude. The whale did a joyous swim in the water. For us humans, I expect if you give it a try, you will find yourself feeling invigorated, and hope has entered in instead of the lowness of heart and mind. So, write down some things to be thankful for. Text, call, or email someone about what you are grateful for, and certainly thank God even if you feel like God didn't come through like you thought He should have. Be mindful that He is at work in your heartache and in everything going on. We have lessons to learn. Don't let being disgruntled be what sinks you.

"He brought them out of darkness and the deepest gloom and broke away their chains" (Psalm 107:14, NIV).

This is to encourage you to go to the Lord with your deepest gloom and that it is Him who has the love and power to break you away from your chains/ropes.

RESPONSE:

_____

_____

_____

_____

_____

_____

_____

_____

_____

_____

_____

_____

_____

_____

_____

_____

_____

_____

_____

_____

_____

_____

DEAR READERS,

We have come to the end, until my next book. I trust you have gained a lot of insight and your life has positively changed. I also wholeheartedly expect that you will continue to learn and grow. May God bless you with His highest and best. I would like to end with this poem that I wrote:

I AM OKAY

My journey isn't over, a lot of progress has been made,

A heavy price was handed me, but many were my aide.

Some memories still haunt and cause me undue pain,

With the Lord's help each step there is a fruitful gain.

There are good days and bad days, He has it all mapped out.

Trying was the first part, then believing and disputing my doubt.

Laughter usually felt funny, but now big smiles often cross my face,

All because I took His hand and accepted His amazing grace.

The numbness has disappeared from the hurts of the past,

Before me is a future, a confident hope that will last.

Goodbye sorrow, go away disgrace, let go heartache,

Onward to a happy life I take the chance to make.

Thank you, Lord for protecting, loving and helping me.

Life, oh life, I am seeing how wonderous things can be.

Patricia I. Tilley, LMHC, 2023

"The Lord is with me like a mighty warrior"
(Jeremiah 20:11, NIV).

Please check out my website at **patriciatilley.com**

Disclaimer:

No skills in this book should be used as a substitute for advice from your doctor or other qualified clinician.

Milton Keynes UK
Ingram Content Group UK Ltd.
UKHW020654290124
436892UK00018B/726